popping the

question

popping the

REAL-LIFE STORIES OF MARRIAGE PROPOSALS

question

FROM THE ROMANTIC TO THE BIZARRE

sheree bykofsky and laurie viera

WALKER AND COMPANY

NEW YORK

First published in the United States of America in 1996 by Walker Publishing
Company, Inc.

Published simultaneously in Canada by Thomas Allen & Son Canada, Limited,
Markham, Ontario

Library of Congress Cataloging-in-Publication Data
Bykofsky, Sheree.
Popping the question: real-life stories of marriage proposals
from the romantic to the bizarre/Sheree Bykofsky and Laurie Viera.
p.   cm.
ISBN 0-8027-7500-4 (pbk.)
1. Marriage proposals.   I. Viera, Laurie.   II. Title.
GT2650.B95   1997
392'.4—dc20   96-28867
CIP

Book design by Chris Welch

Printed in the United States of America

2   4   6   8   10   9   7   5   3   1

contents

acknowledgments

The authors wish to thank the following individuals and companies for their invaluable advice, support, and referrals:

Yoshie Akita, America Online, Rosalind Bykofsky, Rabbi Richard Camras, MaryAnn Carlson, Compuserve, Paulette Cooper, Martha Cronin, Mary Jane Lloyd DeGennaro, Roy Diez, Melitta Fitzer, Layson Fox, Lori Gerson, Angie Golden, Laura Graham, Jennifer Griffin, Linda Gross, Diane Gutterud, Mary Hagen, Aurelia Haslboeck, the Internet, Rachel Klayman, Glenn Lambert, Felice Levine, Sara Levine, Beth Lieberman, Ellen Massey,

Janet Carol Norton, Cary Puma, Janet Rosen, Marilyn Rothstein, Beth Rubens, Rabbi Stuart Seltzer, Celeste Solid, Mike Wolfberg, and our romantic editors at Walker: Liza Miller and Ramsey Walker.

Sheree Bykofsky would like to specially acknowledge Steve Solomon, whose romantic proposal made her cry even before she knew it was a proposal. Thank you, too, Steve, for your editorial help and for making me tea when I was sick.

The authors would like to extend their deepest gratitude to all the people who generously shared their stories with us, and our regrets to those whose stories could not be included in our book. Thank you all for inspiring us with your warmth, humor, humanity, and unfailing belief in the power of love.

introduction

The proposal stories included in these pages are as diverse as the limitless expanse of human experience and personality. The everyday people who shared their betrothal secrets with us come from all walks of life, but there is one thing they have in common. From working stiffs to affluent professionals, city dwellers to small-town citizens, regardless of their shy or sociable temperaments, all of them believe in the power of love and its ability to build a lifelong foundation for happiness.

Writing this book has been an eye-opening odyssey that has never failed to inspire us. In telling their stories the couples were often reminded of what was so special about their early courtship. After many of our interviews, we had not only a renewed faith in the existence of lasting love but also the sense that by sharing their stories, a lot of the couples had inadvertently opened the door to recapturing their own romantic history with each other.

Some of the lovers featured in these pages started out as friends; others felt Cupid's arrow from the moment they met. Some people wanted their proposals to mirror the playfulness and fun that characterized their courtship; others sought to create high drama or to push the envelope of their imaginations. In many of these proposals—almost all of them engineered by men—the proposers took on the courageous roles of writers, directors, and actors in a sort of theatrical play of their own devising. The audience whose approval and admiration they sought to capture consisted of one all-important person: the woman of their dreams. Her favorable reviews would determine the fate of their future together. The elements present in each one-night-only play in this "Theater of the Betrothal" express the unique attributes and eccentricities of each lover, as well as what he or she hoped would please the beloved.

It is our hope that this book will delight and touch you, inspire you with romantic ideas, and afford you a delicious taste of the smorgasbord of ways to ask that life-changing question, "Will you marry me?" Whether you are married or single, jaded in the ways of love or a die-hard romantic, these stories will be sure to enlighten and entertain.

popping the

question

the stuff of fairy tales

a knight in shining armor

Craig and Brigitte, both assistant movie editors, were briefly introduced one day at work, but Brigitte was married at the time. Four years later, they ran into each other again at the studio and were surprised that they remembered their earlier introduction. This was to foreshadow a fateful meeting six months later, when Brigitte showed up at Craig's apartment with his roommate, whom Craig discovered was a friend of hers. Brigitte was in the process of getting a divorce and was interested in renting the third bedroom in Craig's apartment. She moved in but almost immediately left for a Christmas visit to her native France, where she sought the support of her family through this difficult period.

When Brigitte returned, Craig won her heart by throwing her a welcome-home dinner party, complete with elaborately presented delicacies which, he said, "you didn't know whether you should eat or climb." She and Craig became fast friends, and within a month were a good deal more than that.

Brigitte had some reservations: Things seemed to be moving along so quickly, and she was concerned about having a relationship on the rebound. But her doubts were soon dispelled by Craig's sense of romance and humor. Within less than a year, they bought a house together. They didn't specifically discuss marriage, but Craig decided he wanted to propose. He put off his plans, however, until a year later when he could afford an engagement ring.

Craig wasn't sure about Brigitte's ring size, so he waited until she fell asleep one night and put a piece of string around her finger. In her semiconscious state, Brigitte felt someone pulling on her finger and had to stifle a laugh as she realized what Craig must have been up to. Although they hadn't discussed marriage, they both knew they wanted to be together forever. An elaborate proposal, however, was the last thing on her mind.

With the ring ordered and on its way, Craig began to secretly plan and rehearse every minute detail of what was to be an extraordinarily romantic proposal, target date Christmas day. His filmmaking background and love of swashbuckling epics inspired him to stage a romantic scene straight out of the age of knights and damsels. He found a perfect, secluded clearing in Los Angeles' Griffith Park as a location, and reserved a horse for himself at the park's stables. Then he rented a suit of armor and a cape from a well-known Hollywood costume rental house. He even arranged for background music—stirring strains from the soundtrack of *The War Lord* (starring Charlton Heston)—which he would cue up from horseback via a remote-controlled portable boom box hidden behind a tree. He timed the music, figuring he would ride out from behind the tree during the fanfare, then recite a poem during the romantic theme, after which he would descend from the horse and get down on one knee. He even decorated the "set," placing over one hundred small red roses, baby's breath, sweet william, and dried flowers in the evergreens.

But the most challenging task before him was to learn the script for his drama. Craig, an American who spoke not a word of French, was determined to speak words of love to Brigitte in her native language. He obtained a bi-lingual book of French love poetry and chose the poem *"Délie,"* by the sixteenth-century French poet Maurice Scève. A French-speaking friend of Craig's recorded it on tape for him to help him memorize it by rote. For a week Craig walked around with headphones, mumbling to himself in archaic French, like "one of those guys outside 7-Eleven."

The morning of the proposal was almost a disaster for Craig, who had sweated over every small detail. It had stormed the night before, and Craig worried that all his decorations would be washed away. Instead, the flowers had opened and were glistening beautifully, and a light mist gave the clearing a fairy-tale atmosphere. When Craig picked up his horse, the crusty stable manager hardly blinked an eye at the sight of him in all his armorial glory;

however, the "placid, sedentary" horse Craig had requested turned out to be a feisty steed who kept rearing up on its hind legs and threatening to fling its caped rider off its back.

Meanwhile, Brigitte awoke to a tape of Christmas music that Craig had prepared for her and left in the cassette/clock radio. He was long gone, having stayed awake the whole night. (He hadn't figured out a way to get up at 5 A.M. without waking Brigitte.) Craig had also left her a sweet, cryptic note, urging her to meet him in Griffith Park to collect her Christmas present, complete with elaborate directions. Intrigued and excited, but without a clue as to what lay before her, Brigitte arrived at the clearing and, as instructed, called out Craig's name when she saw the tree decked out in red and green ribbons.

Craig was so anxious and preoccupied with getting his horse to calm down that he was unable to practice the poem, but when Brigitte arrived, he started the music and appeared from behind a stand of trees, managing to stay on horseback *and* remember his lines. But, as he said, his reading contained "all the irony and nuance of reading the back of a cereal box." Brigitte didn't even realize that the horse was so troublesome; she only saw that both the horse and Craig were nervous, and, grabbing the bridle, she stroked the horse to calm the two of them. She was too entranced and overwhelmed by being both a spectator and participant in this little drama to be aware of anything else. As for the poem, the ancient form of the French language made it barely intelligible to her ears, but she got the general idea. All she could think was, "This guy is so crazy, he's definitely for me." Refusal was out of the question.

After opening presents that memorable Christmas day,

they went to the St. James' Club, a lovely hotel on Sunset Boulevard, where they had dinner and spent the night.

After Brigitte told their circle of friends about Craig's proposal, the men realized that he would indeed be a hard act to follow.

moon over mulholland

From 1984 to 1988 Clark and Caryn carried on a long-distance relationship: between Pittsburgh and Los Angeles; then New York and Los Angeles, until finally in 1988, they both lived in the same city, New York.

In September of that year, they began to talk about where their relationship was heading, and Clark decided to propose. It was just a matter of when. He remembered Caryn saying that if he were ever to propose, she would

want her parents to know. They laughed at the old-fash-
ioned thought of Clark asking Caryn's father for her hand
in marriage.

The week before Thanksgiving 1989, Caryn took off
for Dallas to visit her brother Randy. She and Clark
planned to rendezvous in Los Angeles on Thanksgiving
day to spend the holiday with Clark's family.

As soon as Caryn left for Dallas, Clark hopped on a
plane to Pittsburgh to see Caryn's parents, Owen and
Shirley. Clark had called Owen and Shirley and said he'd
be in town for the day, but he added that they must not
tell Caryn. He met them for brunch at a Marriott, close to
the airport.

Halfway through the meal, Clark said, "I bet you're
wondering why I've flown all the way out here to meet
you. This may be presumptuous of me, but my brother-
in-law is involved in a big financial deal, and he's looking
for investors, and I'd like to know if you would be interested in investing fifty-thousand dollars in this venture."
He said all this very seriously and straight-faced. They assumed that Clark had arranged this meeting to ask for
Caryn's hand, and now they felt confused and concerned.
All they could do was look at Clark wordlessly.

After letting the silence hang in the air, Clark at last
fessed up: "Actually, that's not why I'm here. I'm looking
to make a different investment—in your daughter's future.
Four days from now I'm planning to ask Caryn to marry
me, and I'd first like to have your blessings."

At this, Shirley started crying tears of joy and relief, and
they all hugged with great happiness and approval. Since
Clark's plane was not to leave for some time, Owen took
Clark to a Steeler's game to celebrate. Unfortunately, the

temperature was fourteen below zero, and Clark, a thin-blooded Los Angeleno, was not prepared. But his new family-to-be made him feel warm and welcomed, and they all had a good time.

Clark flew back to New York that night and telephoned Caryn.

"So, Honey, what did you do today?" she asked.

"Nothing," he lied. "I just cleaned the apartment and took a walk outside. That's about it."

On Wednesday, the day before Thanksgiving, Clark flew to Los Angeles to put the finishing touches on an elaborate plan, with the help of his old friend Beth, a professional party planner. Caryn was not to arrive until the next day.

Caryn had asked Clark if he would pick her up at the airport. Although he didn't intend to do so, he said that he would. He explained, however, that his family was having forty guests for Thanksgiving, so if for some reason he couldn't be at the airport, he would send someone there to meet her.

Caryn was prepared to be picked up, but not by a stretch limo. That certainly took some of the sting out of not having Clark there. Inside the limo, Caryn found on the seat beside her a long-stemmed red rose and a box of Jujyfruits candy in a crystal bowl. The limo driver had been instructed to remove all of the green and black candies (which Caryn doesn't like). According to plan, the limo driver then slipped into the tape deck a cassette compiled by Clark of Caryn's favorite songs.

Just before dusk, the limo cruised along beautiful Mulholland Drive on the way to Clark's parents' house. Still following instructions, the driver explained that he could hear something wrong with the engine and pulled over on top of the hill at the most scenic spot overlooking the San Fernando Valley.

Lo and behold, there was Clark beside a table and two chairs. The table was set with a white tablecloth and two champagne glasses.

A harpist had arrived in a Volvo station wagon, which coincidentally is the same car that Clark's sister drives. In her confusion, Caryn guessed that Clark planned to switch cars so that the family wouldn't give them a hard time about the expensive limo, which they were sure to think was a waste of money. Still, she was unable to rationalize the bizarre scene before her, and she found she couldn't speak.

Clark escorted his bewildered beloved to the table. The limo driver poured them each a glass of champagne. As Clark casually asked Caryn how her weekend was, the harpist played romantic tunes. Caryn remained speechless. The limo driver walked a discreet distance away, and Clark began to tell Caryn how he had gone to see her parents that Sunday past. Ah-ha! Now she knew what was coming next.

Clark handed Caryn a card that said on the outside, "I love you, I want you, I need you." He asked her to open it up, and inside he had written, "Will you marry me?" Then he knelt down and presented her with a little box containing an engagement ring. They both cried as she said, "Yes."

When they recovered, the limo driver packed up the table and drove them to the best Thanksgiving engagement party that anyone ever had.

castles in the sand

In 1988, Thomas and Mary met in their high school study hall. Soon they became fast friends. For six years, despite ups and downs, boyfriends and girlfriends, their friendship never flagged, and on many Sundays they would attend church together.

In 1994, they transferred to the same Alabama college, and in the winter of that year they started dating. But because they had been such good friends for so long, it was an awkward situation for them, and so they didn't tell anyone for months and months. By that time, Thomas got it into his head to propose.

But his proposal wasn't going to be like any other, he decided. Thomas had devised an elaborate plan. The first order of business was to buy the ring. Next, he was determined to ask Mary's father, Jack, for her hand, and he knew he would see Jack that Easter when he and Mary were to visit her parents for the weekend. So Easter it would be.

The plan, as far as Mary knew, was for them to leave school together on Friday night and drive to Mary's folks' house. On Thursday night, Thomas called up Mary to say that he was way too tired to make the journey; there was just no way he could go with her. He told her to go without him and he would arrive on Saturday. Mary was miffed, but what could she do? So off she went by herself on Friday.

Meanwhile, Thomas did leave on Friday. He took the four-and-a-half-hour drive alone, in the middle of the night, arriving at 5 A.M. Saturday morning. He had spent Friday putting the finishing touches on his master plan: He had written something on a sheet of paper, which he burned around the edges so it would look like an old map. This he put into a bottle, which he corked. He did the same thing with another bottle. Then he bought flowers and put champagne on ice.

Arriving at the beach at 5 A.M., Thomas waited many long minutes for a man in a tractor to finish combing the beach to make it even and neat. Thomas's plan was to bury two bottles in case something happened to the first one, or in case someone else found it. Careful to bury each bottle far away from the water, he used markers on the boardwalk to help him remember where his quarry lay. To further mark his spot, Thomas carefully rearranged the debris on the beach, placing a can to the north and a bottle due east.

He then drove to Mary's parents' house. When he arrived at 9 A.M., Mary assumed Thomas had just gotten into town. He was very pleased with himself for being so sneaky without ever having to lie. He still hadn't slept and had been on the road all night, but Mary couldn't tell because Thomas was on an adrenaline high.

Saturday, 11 A.M.: Thomas and Mary sat on the porch talking. Knowing cars bored Mary and any mention of them would drive her away, Thomas announced he had car trouble and asked Mary's dad to look at his vehicle. Mary responded predictably and took refuge inside the house. When Thomas and Jack reached the car, Thomas asked permission to marry Mary. Permission granted, the next phase could now begin.

Saturday, 1 P.M.: Thomas took Mary to the beach. It was a pretty day and warm for April on the scenic Gulf shore. Thomas was a little pickier than usual about where they would put their blankets down. After sunning a while, he said, "Let's build a sand castle." This would give him an excuse to say that evening, "Let's go back to the beach to see if our sand castle is still there." Moreover, he assumed she would not think it so strange to dig around in the sand at night because they would have done it that day. And Thomas discreetly checked that his two bottles were untouched. Mary was a little surprised that Thomas was suddenly so interested in building sand castles, but she wanted to humor him. And so a sand castle they built, a primitive one with no tools, no buckets, no flag, no anything. They worked diligently on it for forty-five minutes. Unbeknownst to Mary, the castle was five feet behind "the spot."

Saturday, 5:30 P.M.: Mary and Thomas went out to dinner with Mary's family, including her parents, aunt, uncle, and grandfather. Only Mary's father knew the secret. During the meal, Mary and her mom were trying to talk Mary's father and Thomas into going dancing. Mary's father said absolutely not. So Thomas and Mary went to a couple of nightclubs alone.

Saturday, 10 P.M.: Thomas asked Mary to take a walk on the beach to see if the sand castle was still there. He did this so smoothly, she felt it was her idea, too. Yes, the sand castle was still there. They sat down on their blanket on the beach. There weren't many people, just a few young teenagers a little way off. Every once in a while, someone would pass by.

Thomas suggested building another sand castle, and they did. By now they had the hang of digging deep into the sand to reach the water that makes it easy for the sand to stick together. As they were digging, Thomas exclaimed, "Wait a minute, I've hit something." Mary went right over to help him dig it up, although she was sure whatever it was would turn out to be just a piece of trash. Finally, they pulled up one of the buried bottles, and he began inspecting it all over, as if only mildly curious. He didn't hand it to her, and not once did he say, "Take a look at this." She was saying, very insistently, "Let me see it, let me see it!"

Finally, he "reluctantly" showed her the bottle. "Oh, it's so cool; what is it?" she said. Thomas pulled out the cork with his teeth and extracted the rolled-up paper, but it was too dark for them to read it. Behind them was the illuminated boardwalk. Thomas casually suggested they go to the boardwalk and read the note. Mary took off running, urging Thomas to hurry. She was bursting to see what the paper said. And so he started reading aloud as Mary scanned it for a date, believing it to be very old indeed.

The letter was a love poem that Thomas had written to Mary, yet even as he read it she didn't know it was for her. Thomas had never written poetry before. In fact, he's more likely to speak of football than Keats. She thought it must have been written by some very romantic sailor out in the ocean to a very lucky woman and was quite touched by this fairy-tale notion. As he finished reading, Mary started to realize something was going on.

Thomas got down on one knee on the boardwalk. The moon was full, and the ocean was peacefully lapping waves onto the shore. Quietly, he asked, "Will you marry me?" They were both shaken by that time, and she said yes about a hundred times. "Yes, yes. I'll marry you." Thomas presented her with the ring and slipped it on her finger. Mary was choked up and crying a little. Thomas does not remember, but Mary does: The teenagers on the beach began to clap. Thomas was completely focused on Mary. He said, "Come here and sit down on the boardwalk. He went to his car and removed the pink roses and champagne. They drank together on the boardwalk and stared at the ocean and the moon. Then together they dug up the other bottle and joked and laughed as he told her the whole story. And off they strolled down the boardwalk, past teenagers, through the moonlight, and right into Easter Sunday.

imagine that!

nothing up my sleeve

After a one-year, long-distance relationship with his girlfriend Julie, Lloyd, a San Francisco Bay Area professional magician and author of books on the paranormal, decided it was time to stop commuting and pop the question using his own, nothing-up-my-sleeve style. He wanted his proposal to surprise, delight, and mesmerize.

Lloyd knew that Julie would say yes, for they had both agreed that marriage was something they wanted in their future. However, Lloyd had deliberately led Julie to believe that before they got engaged, he wanted her to meet his parents, who were not due out from the East Coast for a visit until months later. With true magician showman-ship, Lloyd made sure that he threw Julie completely off track in every way possible.

On one of his trips to Los Angeles to visit her, Lloyd took his beloved to one of their favorite restaurants, a lit-tle-known but fabulous place called Joe's Steak Pit. Lloyd knew the owners, and, before he picked Julie up for their date, he stopped by the restaurant and dropped off a gor-geous bouquet of roses and a bottle of champagne.

During their dinner at a secluded corner table, Lloyd told Julie he wanted to show her a couple of new magic tricks he'd worked out. This was a routine and enjoyable scenario in their relationship, because Lloyd was con-stantly improving his magician skills and testing them out on Julie. After a couple of entertaining card tricks, Lloyd performed a cup-and-ball trick, in which a cup is lifted up to reveal a ball, then lifted up again to show that the ball has disappeared, then again to reveal a rubber eye, and so forth. Lloyd lifted up the cup a final time. This time a new object was revealed—a ring.

Now this wasn't just any sort of ring; it was a poison ring, the type that has a locket-type chamber in which deadly powders and potions can be stored and surrepti-tiously slipped into your unsuspecting companion's drink. Julie saw, to her surprise, that around the ring was a tiny tag, *Alice in Wonderland*–style, with an inscription that said, "OPEN ME." She opened up the ring, and inside was an even tinier scroll. She unrolled the tiny scroll, and, in-scribed in the most minuscule print imaginable, were those four magical words: "WILL YOU MARRY ME?"

Julie was stunned, for this was the last thing she ex-pected to see. Touched by this sweet, romantic gesture,

and already sure about wanting a future with Lloyd, Julie said yes. Lloyd signaled to the waiter, who then brought over the roses and champagne.

When asked if he intended to pull any tricks at his wedding, Lloyd said probably not, but who knows? He certainly wouldn't ruin a surprise by telling this author.

HOT TIP FOR LOVERS WHO WANT A MAGICAL PROPOSAL: Lloyd encourages even those lovers with no experience in magic to visit their local magic shop. Most magic dealers would be happy to show them tricks that are easy and inexpensive (under twenty-five dollars), and that, with a little practice, will create the desired effect.

hawaiian surprise

Stu Bykofsky, a wisecracking columnist for the *Philadelphia Daily News*, had been around the dating block enough times in the eighteen years since his divorce to know that after seven years with his comedian girlfriend Maria Merlino, it couldn't get any better than this. They'd never even discussed marriage, but Stu figured that it was high time he proposed. He decided to make his proposal to Maria a surprise. Better yet, he decided to fast-forward things and make the *wedding* a surprise, too.

Stu and Maria were planning on vacationing in Australia, and their itinerary included a two-day stopover in Honolulu on the way back to Philadelphia. From Stu's mission-control desk at the newspaper as well as from Australia, he began launching every minute detail of his secret plan for a surprise Hawaiian wedding. He confided in only a few people, including his close female colleague and friend Mary Flannery, whom Stu affectionately refers to as his "office spouse." At first aghast when she heard of Stu's brilliant idea for a surprise wedding, Mary soon became fond of the idea, offering helpful suggestions on how to make the event as romantic as possible. Stu also let his editor know, a clever move which resulted in not only a lovely bottle of Cristal champagne, but reimbursement for many of Stu's wedding expenses when his editor insisted that Stu write a column about the wedding upon his return to the paper.

The only other person to whom Stu revealed his wedding plans was a very close male friend, because Stu needed his help in picking out a wedding ring. Stu figured out the proper size of the ring by slipping one of Maria's rings on his pinky, and noting how far down on his finger it fit. With wedding ring in hand, Stu tackled the next obstacle.

Luckily, Hawaii does not make couples take a blood test, but it does require a rubella certificate. Stu called Maria's doctor and told him that he needed the certificate so Maria could travel to Australia. Pretty clever, but what about the marriage license? Because the state of Hawaii thrives on tourism, the license registry was very accommodating: Technically, a couple must sign the license prior to the wedding, but the registry bent the rules. It even offered to send one of its clerks to the hotel at the time the wedding was to take place, and the clerk actually waited in the wings until the ceremony was concluded, at which time Maria was asked to sign. The charge for such a service, not to mention on a weekend? A mere twenty bucks.

The Sheraton Moana Surfrider's public relations director Barbara Sheehan couldn't have been more helpful to Stu concerning the wedding arrangements. She coordinated everything from hiring the minister to providing the services of her four-year-old daughter as flower girl. She arranged traditional wedding leis and a wedding cake, all conforming to Stu's exact specifications. (He admits he's a bit of a control freak, but after all, this was his wedding.)

The only hitch in Stu's flawless surprise was when they arrived at the Sheraton in Honolulu and Stu found their accommodations had been upgraded to a minisuite, courtesy of the hotel. Stu passed this perk off as part of the package he'd booked for them. Maria was thrilled with the room, but puzzled when she saw in an ashtray a book of matches and a pad of hotel stationery engraved with the names "Mr. & Mrs. Bykofsky." Without missing a beat, Stu coolly explained that he'd booked the vacation package for "Mr. & Mrs. Bykofsky" to make things simpler. No problem. Maria bought it without a second thought.

While Maria rested in the room, Stu slipped out to make sure everything was in place. They had plans to eat in the hotel's signature restaurant that night, but first, Stu offered to buy Maria a Hawaiian dress to wear to dinner. She was a bit surprised when Stu bought himself a matching shirt, for, as he says, he's "not into twins." Besides, the last time they were in Hawaii together and wore matching shirts, she was barely able to restrain her loved one from beating up a teenager who poked fun at them for being too cute for words.

At 6 P.M., decked out in their matching Hawaiian dinner garb, Stu walked Maria out onto the hotel terrace to check out the spectacular view of Diamond Head. The hotel had reassigned its lobby musicians to terrace duty for the occasion, and when the band struck up the tune "Maria," Stu dropped to one knee and proposed. A man who Maria assumed was a Japanese tourist started taking pictures of the couple, but actually he was a photojournalist whom Stu had booked to immortalize the event.

Maria didn't say yes right away, for she couldn't stop giggling. But Stu insisted on an answer, as the pebbly surface of the terrace floor was doing a number on his knee. She said yes and smiled, and immediately a man in a suit walked over to the couple and began talking to them in flowery terms about eternal love and the beauty of the islands. Maria was confused, thinking that perhaps he was the manager of the hotel waxing poetic about this exotic tourist spot. She was also wondering why the "manager" was holding the guest book. Did he want them to sign it? The "guest book" was, in fact, a Bible, and about a minute into the "manager's" speech, it hit her that she was getting married. Maria was so overcome with emotion that she didn't know whether to laugh or cry, so she did both.

The ceremony concluded, the newly married couple kissed, champagne and cake were brought out, and the license was signed. The small wedding party, which consisted of Barbara Sheehan and a few hotel employees, the minister, photographer, and marriage license clerk, had a piece of cake and toasted Stu and Maria. The couple then had a beautiful dinner in the hotel's restaurant, and Stu basked in the glory of a flawlessly romantic plan that went off without a hitch.

Why did Stu dream up a surprise wedding with only a handful of strangers as guests? Aside from his certainty that Maria would say yes and the suitability of an idyllic romantic setting, Stu spared himself and his beloved the inevitable hassles and familial pressures that accompany most nuptials.

the case of the caring cartoonist

Although he is unassuming and a bit self-deprecating, John is a well-known figure in Madison, Wisconsin, where every day he dreams up a new installment for his popular and widely distributed comic strip "Wild Life," a strip he created and has drawn since he was in high school. "Wild Life" is not only published in Madison's paper, the *Wisconsin State Journal*, but also in various other newspapers, as well as on the Internet.

One night, John was asked to be a "celebrity waiter" for a charity gala. Judith, a beautiful woman who had worked with John seven years before at the University of Wisconsin at Madison's student newspaper, the *Daily Cardinal,* happened to be sitting at a nearby table. Although she hadn't seen John in seven years, she recognized him instantly, and asked her waiter to call him over.

John was flattered that Judith remembered him, for she was someone he'd secretly admired in their college days. Unfortunately for John, she had a boyfriend back then, a big boyfriend, bigger than John. That was pretty unusual for John, who is six-foot-four. Nevertheless, he wasn't about to vie for Judith's affections with a giant college football player, especially because at the time he had absolutely no idea that Judith liked him, too. If he had known, he says, he "would have leaped at her."

Although he was brokenhearted over a very recent and painful breakup, the night John saw Judith at that charity benefit his first thought was that maybe this breakup wasn't such a bad thing after all, not if a gorgeous woman in a killer red dress wanted to meet him. He didn't have the nerve to ask her out, however. After he finished work, he hung out in the adjacent bar with some of his "media geek" friends. At that point, one of the women he'd waited on at dinner came up to him and gave him her phone number. This confirmation of John's attractiveness gave him the courage to ask Judith for her address so that he could send her some of the comic strip books he'd published.

He did send the books the very next day and found that he couldn't get Judith out of his mind. They quickly began dating, and although John was crazy about Judith, he still had a lot of baggage from his prior relationship. He was completely honest with Judith about his situation, and told her there was a chance that he might get back together with his ex, who was lobbying for just that opportunity. Had it not been for Judith, John probably would have resumed seeing his former girlfriend.

Judith was amazingly patient throughout John's ups and downs, even when John decided to take time off from seeing her to sort things out for himself. Judith felt confident that he would, and sure enough, John began to realize that the exciting, yet easy and comfortable relationship he had with Judith was something he didn't want to lose. When they got back together, he was able to devote himself to her wholeheartedly.

As the two-year anniversary of their relationship approached, John decided to propose. Although they'd never discussed marriage, they both knew that after all they'd been through together, their love would last forever. John wanted his proposal to be something special, something that was distinctly his own.

The day before their two-year anniversary, John remembered that when they started dating, Judith showed John an original comic strip drawing he'd given her seven years before and she'd kept all these years, as proof of her earlier affections. What better way to pop the question than through his comic strip, whose Carson the Muskrat character is essentially John's alter ego? John had already written the strip that was to come out on his anniversary, but drove back to the paper and asked his managing editor's permission to change it for the next day's local newspaper edition. He didn't offer any details, because he didn't want to run the risk of being turned down.

As John redrew the comic strip, his hand was literally shaking. He couldn't draw it fast enough. He felt confident that Judith would say yes, but he was still a nervous wreck. If she did say no, he comforted himself with the fact that he'd have plenty of new material for the next several comic strips.

The comic strip proposal appeared in the next morning's paper, and John was astonished by the reaction around town. He started getting calls from local radio disc jockeys at six in the morning, before Judith had even seen the newspaper. Worried that Judith might hear about his proposal on the radio, John turned off her clock radio. When John went into his home office to work, Judith turned it back on, only to hear her proposal read on the air by John Irvin, her favorite morning DJ.

In the strip, Carson reads from a page, "My love for you is ever true, and greater, far, than any sea. You are my joy, my light, my life . . . Judith, will you marry me?—

John." Judith had expected that John would pull off some sort of romantic surprise for their anniversary, but she never expected this. After her initial shock, Judith told John what she'd just heard. They held each other tightly, and Judith said, "Of course I'll marry you."

John then showed Judith the paper, and the rest of the morning was spent on the phone letting friends, family, and, of course, the inquisitive radio stations know that she had indeed said yes. In fact, John Irvin, the radio DJ who read the comic strip on the air, was the DJ at John and Judith's wedding. They thought this was only fitting, since it was Irvin's voice that proposed to Judith.

John's proposal became a local media event, with both the *Wisconsin State Journal* and the competing newspaper writing stories about it. John's not so sure his managing editor loved the comic strip's ending, however, when Snyder the Badger comments on the difficulty one might experience trying to buy a ring on a *Wisconsin State Journal* salary.

Everyone in Madison was talking about Judith and John that special day, and they've gotten letters and phone calls from all over the country. But the best part about it for John was all the attention it brought to Judith. Her home-town newspaper even made it front-page news. John wants it on the record, though, that the *National Enquirer*'s quote that "tears of joy were streaming down [their] cheeks" is a fabrication.

John feels incredibly lucky to have found Judith, who stood by him through the whole process of recovering from his past relationship. Now his biggest challenge is to keep Carson in character, for John's humble comic strip alter ego never even gets a date.

the amorous animator

Tracy and Ronald lived parallel lives. They both grew up in Cincinnati, although they never met there. Their mothers went to the same college at the same time and also never met. Tracy and Ronald both moved to New York and attended classes on Saturday mornings during the same semester at the Art Student's League. With all that, though, they would have continued to remain ignorant of each other's existence had Tracy not gone home to Cincinnati to spend Thanksgiving with her family.

Tracy's father, a retired jeweler, still did repair jobs for friends. When a customer named Eddie stopped by Tracy's father's house that Thanksgiving to pick up a piece of jewelry, he took one look at Tracy and got a notion to set Tracy up with Ronald, his friend's son who lived in New York.

Would it be OK for Ronald to call Tracy? Tracy didn't mind. She was about to start a new job as a senior editor at a large publishing house and was very wrapped up in her career. She didn't really care if it worked out or not, so why not? And lo and behold, Ronald called.

They met for a drink, and they immediately liked each other—a lot. And, it turned out, they had much in common. They had been circling around each other all these years, and they had to come all the way to New York to finally meet.

In time they became an item, and marriage became an inevitable topic of conversation. But those discussions usually ended with Ronald asking, "Should I do it? Should I do it?" Tracy, less than impressed, would respond, "A girl likes to be asked." They chose to focus on their careers, and consequently the discussion never advanced beyond these preliminary feelers.

Tracy was fascinated by Ronald's career. He does animation for motion picture special effects. When Ronald animates a film, he does it by hand, using dozens and dozens—in fact often hundreds—of painstaking drawings.

Two years after they met, Tracy visited the studio to watch Ronald work. He had been working very long hours on a wild science fiction film that involved an alien monster. Now he was animating a sequence involving a lot of lightning and sparks—more sparks than Tracy could possibly know.

When they saw the movie together in November, Tracy was captivated by a scene where the heroes had cornered the alien in a meatpacking plant and turned the sprinkler system on him. Because the alien was electrically wired, he was shorting out. This was Tracy's favorite scene, and she knew how much work had gone into it.

Tracy also knew that Ronald often puts his signature in one frame of his animation as a way of marking it as his own, just as a painter would sign a landscape. But Tracy did not know where in this film Ronald had hidden his name. Technically, one second of a movie contains twenty-four frames. Ronald would hide his signature in a single frame of film, and you would have to stop the film at one twenty-fourth of a second to see it.

That Christmas in Cincinnati, Ronald found a moment to be alone with Tracy in his family's house. He said, "I have something for you." He pulled out his portfolio and showed her some blowups of single frames of his sparks animation from the science fiction film. He said, "Do you know what this is?" She responded, "Yeah, one frame of your animation." Turning the page, Tracy expected to find Ronald's name, but she found something quite different: On a single frame of film from Tracy's favorite scene in the meatpacking plant, you could read in the sparks the words "marry me."

Tracy was thrilled and surprised. She never expected to be proposed to like that. And so it came to be that Tracy went all the way to New York (and Hollywood!) to marry

the boy next door. She knows that for now and always—
even after she is gone—every time the movie is played,
Ronald's proposal lives on, flashing on the screen faster
than the eye can see.

And consider this: The next time you're watching a
movie, you or somebody next to you just might be getting
a proposal of their own.

chairman of the nba

Brad, Jennifer, and Lisa were three best friends. Almost
everything they did, they did as a threesome: Super Bowl
parties, holiday meals, movies, and evenings of games and
Melrose Place. One for three and three for one—that is,
until that fateful Valentine's Day, a holiday they cynically
referred to as "Black Monday."

In defiance of the holiday, Brad elected to cook dinner
for his two friends. They all wore black. And Brad made
Valentine cards for both of them. Lisa's was all about
friendship. Jenn's was a poem that he printed in the shape
of a diamond on his computer:

Formed
of such del-
icate constitu-
tion, yet having a
profoundly uplifting
effect on those who en-
counter it, the rose is one of
nature's finest works. The sweet-
ness of its bouquet evokes wondrous
images of perfect spring days; perhaps a
heavenly stroll through magnificently col-
ored gardens; birds circling incessantly over-
head, almost as if they're unable to abandon such a
fantastic display of fragrance and color. That such over-
whelming feelings of happiness and comfort can be
aroused by any singular creation is almost in-
conceivable, yet it happens every time.
Every encounter revitalizing those
who make the time to experience
the wonders of the rose . . .
kind of reminds me of
someone I know. . . .
Happy Valen-
tine's Day.

He signed the card with a handwritten line: "I can't tell you how fortunate I feel to know you. Love, Brad."

Brad had only just begun to think about asking Jenn out on a date, but he was still in a state of denial about his deeper feelings for her. And until this moment Jenn herself was completely clueless.

The next day Lisa called Brad and asked if Jenn's card was meant to be romantic. Brad said he didn't know but did admit to wanting to ask Jenn out. Lisa was thrilled and gave her blessing. She then called Jenn to relate the news.

Jenn was thrown into a state of anxiety. "I can't go out with him. I can't!" They were all such good friends, and Jenn was scared that everything was going to change. When Brad finally asked Jenn himself, she put him off at first, but before long had a change of heart and agreed. They both knew this was going to be not just a date but the beginning of a relationship, and they hoped it would not be the end of a wonderful friendship. In fact, Brad said it was not just a date he wanted, but to begin "seeing her," to start a relationship. This was a proposal in itself. And Jenn finally felt comfortable with the idea.

Brad wanted to ensure that their first date would be perfect. He thought they would go ice skating and then to a restaurant. That afternoon, he made a trial run: He drove the route to the skating rink. But when he got there, he saw 150 people in line for skates with no skates left to rent. This would not do. The whole date was shot, he thought. He had to come up with a new plan.

So Brad decided to take Jenn to the bowling alley, which he checked out in advance, and to a nice restaurant, and then to the theater. Then they returned to her house to watch *Saturday Night Live*. All night long, Brad's hand was on his leg with his palm turned up to give her a chance to hold it, but he complains today that she never noticed that. Their first date wasn't much different from their previous friendly outings. They didn't kiss goodnight, and Jenn felt bad about that. It wasn't until the next day when they went fishing that they had their first kiss, and it broke the ice. They started to see each other every day and soon became so publicly mushy together that it made other people, including Lisa, feel awkward. Such is the price of love.

They talked about everything: their thoughts, feelings, hopes, dreams, and what they wanted out of life and their relationship. They examined it all like a couple of scientists, and Brad thinks that's why things worked out so well for them.

They went on a seven-day trip to Colorado, and the whole time they talked about moving in together or getting married. Jenn said to Brad, "I could marry you." It was the greatest vacation they'd ever had. On the seventh day they returned to their jobs. Brad was an estimator at a manufacturing plant, and Jenn was a special education teacher at a junior high school for intelligent children with emotional problems.

Brad thought he might like to propose to Jenn at a school assembly. The school principal told him that no assemblies were scheduled until much later in the year, but that if Brad wanted to propose over the school's TV system at the end of the day, he could do so at any time (each class has a TV to watch channel one, the educational channel). Knowing he would have the ring by then, Brad picked September sixteenth as the date to propose.

On the evening of September fifteenth, Jenn roped Brad into baby-sitting with her. He couldn't tell her he had other plans. After he left Jenn, he dashed home to put on a suit and tie and then raced with his camcorder to his Dad's boardroom. He was up very late into the night preparing his proposal.

On the morning of the sixteenth, Brad called the school to finalize his plan. There were many people in on it: the school secretary, the principal, the vice principal, Jenn's teaching mentor, Paula, and some video class students who were going to videotape Jenn's reaction using the pretext of practicing their skills. While Brad was speaking at length to the school secretary about the plan, the secretary suddenly said, "Here's Jenn; she's right here, talk to her," and Brad thought the best cover would be to make Jenn jealous. He said, "Nothing, we weren't talking about anything. Just forget it." Not convinced, Jenn said, "Fine. Bye," and stormed off. This was their first little fight, but he wasn't going to have his proposal ruined because the school secretary had slipped up for a moment.

It was a stealthy operation involving minute-by-minute monitoring and planning. Brad had to sit outside the school for about twenty minutes and wait with a cell phone in his car, calling every two minutes to find out when Jenn would go into her room to teach. Then the vice principal led Brad into the principal's office, where he had to wait another fifteen while they played the video.

The moment came. Jenn sat down expecting to see the usual educational news on the screen. What she saw was Brad sitting at the end of a long boardroom table with a glass fishbowl in front of him. In the bowl was a single piece of paper.

At first she didn't recognize him. For one thing, he was in a suit. She sat back into her chair saying, "Oh my gosh. It's Brad." What she saw on the TV screen was this: Using a prepared speech, he said, "Hi, my name is Brad Emmons, and I'm chairman of the NBA, the National Bachelor's Association. For the past eight years I have fulfilled my duties faithfully and with great vigor, but I believe it's come time for me to resign and no longer be a bachelor.

It's time for me to settle down and find a woman to marry. Over the past four years I have employed the greatest research marketing firm in the country to scour the earth with a list of criteria that I gave them to find the perfect woman, the woman that deserves to marry the chairman of the NBA." Brad grabbed the fishbowl, tilted it toward the camera, and proceeded: "This is all the women who met the criteria that I gave them. We'll now do a lottery drawing to see what lucky woman gets to marry me, Brad Emmons, chairman of the National Bachelor's Association." He closed his eyes and, turning his head away, ran his hand around the inside of the bowl a few times. Finally, he removed the piece of paper that was in it, unfolded the paper, and said, "The lucky woman is Jennifer Gallagher. Jennifer Gallagher, will you marry me?" Then, while pointing to the door, he added, "I should be coming in about now."

And that's what happened. The real Brad, dressed in the same suit, walked through the door into the classroom carrying a rose and Jenn's ring. He handed her the rose and put the ring on her finger. The students needed her reply. They tapped their feet impatiently, saying, "Well, well . . . ?" All over the school, students and teachers were cheering wildly—some were crying. "What did she say? What did she say?" they asked. As soon as Jenn realized she was being proposed to, out came her happy reply: "Yes!" The bell rang, and all eight hundred people at the junior high came racing to Jenn's room to congratulate the happy couple.

Brad says, "When you start out as friends, in order to make it worth the risk of losing the friendship, you've got to make it good. It's got to be extremely special." The couple kissed as they told us their story.

the adventures of coojy and manley

Before he began to work freelance in March of 1984, Colin worked for a London company that produced corporate videos. Claudia joined the company in June, after Colin's departure. Shortly thereafter, on the eve of Colin's twenty-sixth birthday, the office gang invited Colin back to share a meal with the staff in a nearby restaurant. Colin and Claudia became instant friends that night but did not start dating until August fifteenth.

For a while, Claudia lived with her parents in Brighton, an hour away, before deciding that she needed to be closer to the company. At about the same time she was deciding to move closer to the company, Colin also found himself in need of a new place to live. Because they had become such good friends, Colin and Claudia decided to look for a house to share. They ended up in a five-way share that they say became one of the best house shares in history. It wasn't long before Claudia and Colin became lovers.

Claudia's boss, Brian, was set in his ways, and Claudia and Colin did not think he would be sympathetic if he knew that one of his freelancers was "off snogging"* a member of his staff. He would probably stop using Colin's freelance services if he knew, so they decided to keep their relationship a secret from him. It was about a year before Brian found out, long after everyone in the crew became aware of the romance.

*Snogging is heavy kissing, such as would be carried out by courting couples and not by auntie and nephew.

One day Claudia went with Brian to a TV studio for a two-day shoot. The two were staying in a hotel near the studio, where she and Colin had arranged for Colin to stay the night as an unregistered guest.

Colin arrived under the cover of darkness. Clandestine phone calls were exchanged from the phone box down the road. Claudia stole away to the fire exit, and Colin made a very quiet entrance. They crept down the hall to their room and slipped into bed.

It was only minutes later that the fire alarm went off. A quick peek out of the window revealed smoke pouring from a few floors below. Claudia and Colin were in a state of panic. Not only was Colin "illegal," but he was extremely likely to bump into Brian in the corridor!!!

The lovers evacuated to separate areas. Claudia joined the other guests at the assembly point, and Colin kept watch on the proceedings from beneath the shade of a large tree. It was only a small fire in the kitchen, and it was put out before the fire brigade arrived. Meanwhile, Brian had heard the alarm but couldn't be bothered to get out of bed!

Claudia and Colin cohabited for two and a half years in the house share, but they had separate rooms for the sake of visiting parents. They couldn't afford a double bed, so they slept on two single mattresses pushed together in Claudia's room. When she visited, Colin's mother expressed concern about Colin sleeping on a bed with no mattress, and Claudia and Colin were always giggling about falling down the crevice every time the two mattresses parted.

In time they bought a house together, and then they bought another. Although they, especially Claudia, were thinking about marriage, they decided not to, because there was a mortgage law that made it far more advantageous economically to own the house together without being married. Once the law changed, however, Claudia started dropping hints.

Colin will tell you he enjoys being "a minor noncomformist," so you can be sure that dropping down on one knee at a fancy restaurant was not going to do the trick for him. He had to come up with something else. Well, it seems Claudia was given a Teddy bear when she was very small by her Uncle Phil. She called the bear Coojy and it was her favorite—he moved in with Colin when Claudia did. After Claudia and Colin were together, Uncle Phil (now deceased) gave her another bear, which Colin christened Manley.

When Claudia had trouble sleeping at night after a very stressful day at work, Colin would make up bedtime stories about Coojy and Manley's "adventures." The bears, for example, would be on a sunny beach where they would use giant soft marshmallows as pillows. These were just the normal fantasy things that stuffed bears do when we humans are not looking or are asleep. There was always a silly element to the stories, and they never failed to get a giggle or two out of Claudia.

Colin thought Christmas would be a good time to propose and started to make his plan in the fall. He spent two full days carrying out his plan while Claudia was out. What he did was pose the bears in different situations and photograph them so that he could arrange them into a book with a story. He says it's amazing what you can do with a bear with a wire coathanger up its back. It's possible that

Claudia may have noticed a grubby paw, but Colin left no other clues.

We'll let Colin tell you what happened next: "The photographs came back after a couple of clandestine visits to the processors. I then used the computer to do a posh bit of word processing to make up the very simple text. I stuck the pickies [pictures] on the paper and went to a print shop to have a comb binder put in. I thought I would give it to her on Christmas day.

"On Christmas eve we were baking a rich chocolate cake. After it was mixed, we realized we didn't have a tin big enough to bake it in, so Claudia thought of a wizard wheeze [good plan or idea]. She took the biggest tin we had and made an extension for it out of greaseproof paper. Oh calamity—it wasn't until it was well under way that it became apparent that before the ingredients could cook together, they had to melt together! Yuk, what a mess. I had to strip the oven down completely to clean it up, and there were tears well before bedtime as the planned pudding plonked into the bin! Claudia was much depressed as a replacement was considerably difficult at this late stage. To cheer her up a bit, I gave her the book and she laughed at it through tears, worked out the final 'a rag man' (anagram of 'anagram'), and said 'Yes.' "

a sign of love

When Skippy moved in with her boyfriend, Manny, marriage was the last thing on her mind. She was separated

from her first husband, had four children living with her, and was facing an extremely acrimonious divorce. When the divorce was final, Manny mentioned the "m" word, but Skippy couldn't go through with it. It wasn't that she had a problem with marriage; she had a problem with divorce, and that was something she definitely didn't want to do again. She even resisted entreaties from Manny's financial manager, who warned her that if Manny died unmarried, Skippy would have to pay heavy estate taxes in order to inherit Manny's property. If she were his wife, however . . . Feigning offense, Skippy asked the manager if he were suggesting she marry Manny for his money. Not *his* money, the manager insisted, *your* money!

Skippy agreed that if Manny were to get really, really sick, she'd marry him. But what would happen if he recovered? she innocently asked Manny. He told her not to worry; he promised to divorce her should such an unfortunate miracle occur. All of this was small comfort for Manny, who realized that if he should ever end up in a hospital bed and see his beloved arrive with a minister, he was basically a dead man.

Despite all the gallows humor, Manny was unshaken in his determination to marry Skippy, and to live to enjoy marital life. Finally, she relented: If he asked her properly, she'd consider it. Manny wasn't about to leave himself open to rejection, and insisted on knowing what her answer would be, should he figure out a way to ask her "properly." Skippy promised she'd say yes.

For the next month, Skippy perused announcements in the *New York Times* for proposals and scanned the skies for skywriting, but nothing applied to her. One rainy Friday night while Manny was out of town on business, Skippy was cozy at home with the children when her girlfriend phoned and said, "So what are you gonna say?" Skippy didn't know what her friend was talking about, and when she persisted, Skippy figured she must have been drinking. "Eighty-ninth and First," her friend insisted. At this point, Skippy hung up the phone, exasperated.

The next interruption came in the form of Skippy's mother, who appeared at Skippy's door in a raincoat and insisted that Skippy get in a cab and go to Eighty-ninth and First. Reluctantly, Skippy ventured out in the rain, informing the cabbie that she was going to Eighty-ninth and First, and earning his professional scorn when she admitted she didn't have an address. When they reached that particular corner, however, she couldn't help but see a gigantic billboard painted with rainbows and bearing the words: "SKIPPY, I'M ASKING." Astonished, Skippy told the cabbie to pull over, that the billboard was what she was looking for. Roused out of his usual New York indifference, the cabbie looked at his fare with new interest and said, "Are you Skippy, lady?" When she dazedly nodded her assent, the cabbie sagely advised, "I don't know what he's asking, lady, but you'd better do it." She did.

After such a grandiose offer of marriage, the couple decided to have a small, private civil ceremony at a registrar's office in Edinburgh, Scotland. Manny arranged a small surprise for his bride, however, in the form of two hired men marching down the registrar's little side street wearing sandwich boards that proclaimed, "SKIPPY, THANKS FOR ANSWERING," along with an extremely tall Scottish piper serenading the couple as they entered the office.

As the newly married couple emerged from the registrar's, both Manny and his bride were unprepared for a stunt pulled by Manny's colleague, who had leaked the billboard story to the Edinburgh press. No fewer than twenty-five reporters, including TV cameras, surrounded the couple, eager to know if Manny was simply a millionaire or a multimillionaire. All of them were dying to know how much the billboard cost (Manny no longer remembers). Meanwhile, a rumor had spread around Edinburgh that a "rock star" was getting married (Manny is an investment banker), and as soon as the couple got past the reporters, they were greeted by throngs of curious Scots. So much for a quiet wedding.

Fourteen years later, Manny and Skippy celebrated their anniversary with a huge party, the invitations proclaiming with typical comic flair that their relationship had spanned twenty years, eighteen of which were the happiest of their lives.

the gift

Houston, 1981. Maura happened to be showing her visiting sister a real country and western bar on the same night that Keith was showing his old college friend the same kind of good time. Maura and Keith locked eyes with each other across the dance floor, and he asked her to dance.

They danced for quite a while that night and many nights after that. Often they would go on nature walks, to the zoo, to restaurants. Yes, life together in Houston was good, and in 1984, when Keith bought a house in Louisiana, Maura moved, too.

Maura knew she wanted to marry Keith, and she was getting a little impatient waiting for him to decide. But by 1984 they were thinking and talking a little bit more about marriage and making a long-term commitment.

Maura was very close with her family, and she would often go to visit them in Massachusetts. Usually Keith would accompany her, but during Christmas of 1985, he just couldn't go. However, he managed to hatch a proposal plan that would allow him to be with Maura even though he was home alone.

While Keith was working out his plan, Maura's Dad was saying to the family that if Keith didn't show up next time with a ring, he didn't have to bother showing up at all. Keith learned about this proclamation only *after* the engagement, so he guesses his timing was fortunate.

Keith figured that Maura would enjoy being proposed to if she could share the moment with her friends and family, but a telephone proposal wouldn't do. He bought a silver candlestick, a white candle, and a diamond ring. He lined a white box with pillow stuffing and black velvet. In it he placed the candle in the candlestick. And over the candle he placed the ring. Beside the candle he taped down a pewter bookmark, engraved with the words "Will You Marry Me?" He wrapped the box in Christmas paper.

When Maura was leaving for Massachusetts, Keith gave her the box as her Christmas gift. She asked, "Is there anything special in here?" to which he answered, "No, you can just check it with your luggage." And she did. Maura wasn't expecting anything at all out of the ordinary.

Christmas morning at Maura's family's home was always a big production. The elaborately decorated house resounded with laughter as everyone joked, teased each other, and talked. The family gathered as always around the tree: Maura, her parents, three sisters, her brother, and her brother-in-law, all tearing open their presents in a merry sort of chaos.

When Maura opened Keith's big box, all she saw was the candle and the pewter bookmark. She realized she was actually being proposed to. Luckily, Maura's sister said, "Wait a minute, there's got to be a ring in there somewhere," and Maura started throwing things out of the box until she found the ring.

Maura was very, very happy and shocked, and her whole family was surprised. The only ones who had known of the proposal were Keith, the jeweler, and the engraver. Within minutes, Maura called Keith to say yes, she would marry him. As Keith had known, it was all right with Maura that he was far away. He knew her well enough to know that it would be more important for her to be with her family than with him at that moment. Marriage was something that she really wanted, while Keith had been a dyed-in-the-wool bachelor for many years. Marriage and family had been foreign concepts to him, but he knew that for Maura they were everything.

That was then. Now, Maura keeps the bookmark with her wedding album, and they're raising two boys in the house that Keith bought. They have lots of friends in town, but Keith just got transferred to Pittsburgh where they are now starting anew.

peculiar proposals

ain't no water deep enough, baby

Christine, a bookkeeper, and her boyfriend Steve, a printer, enjoyed scuba diving and snow skiing together whenever time and money allowed. Steve had dropped huge hints to Christine's parents a couple of months before about proposing, so Christine's father Roy had an idea that Steve would pop the question on an upcoming family diving excursion.

Christine, however, had no such suspicions. She and Steve had decided they both wanted to get married, but Christine told Steve that she didn't want anything resembling what had happened between Steve and a former girlfriend. That young woman had basically demanded a ring as a solution to a troubled relationship, which definitely did not save the liaison from its inevitable failure. Christine wanted a romantic proposal, and she wanted to be surprised. This would definitely be a challenge for Steve, who had never been adept at keeping secrets from his sweetheart. Christine invariably made correct guesses about all of Steve's gifts and surprises, because his hints were so obvious.

For this reason, she had been certain that Steve was going to propose to her when he insisted they take a last-minute Colorado ski trip, a trip he said they'd never be able to afford again once they got married. When he didn't propose on the slopes, she had felt somewhat confused and disappointed.

A few months later, Christine and Steve, along with her father Roy, her brother, and another couple, took a diving expedition to a hauntingly beautiful underwater site about a half hour outside St. Louis. This enchanting place was once a thriving lead mine which was literally flooded into retirement. Here, in crystal-clear water, Christine and Steve's group explored caves and viewed dramatic rock formations, sparkling white crystals, and miners' ore carts, all illuminated by huge underwater lights.

When the group finished their dive, Christine was surprised to hear the dive master say he would take her group down a second time, for she had been told that they would only be allowed to make one dive on this trip. Nonetheless, she was excited to be going underwater again and was completely unaware that Steve had arranged the whole thing with the dive master to aid him in his amorous intentions.

So how, you may ask, does one propose underwater

with a regulator in one's mouth? It's not as difficult as it might seem. At one point while exploring underwater, the dive master pointed his flashlight at Christine to get her attention. She turned toward the beam of light and saw Steve, who handed her his underwater slate. On it, in big waterproof chalk letters, were written the words, "Will you marry me?" Stunned, and aware of the verbal limitations presented by a regulator in her mouth, Christine momentarily looked blankly at Steve. Collecting herself, she finally nodded her head in the affirmative. Steve excitedly grabbed her gloved hand in his own, and slipped a child's expandable ring on her gloved ring finger.

Their little group of wet-suited witnesses proceeded to hug the newly betrothed couple, and took their regulators out of their mouths to joyously scream underwater. Christine declined to join in for fear of swallowing water, even when Steve removed his own regulator to give her an engagement kiss.

Christine was still recovering from her shock as the group swam up toward the surface. She was the last one to emerge from the water, and was so preoccupied with recent events that she ended up getting whacked in the head with a fellow diver's fin. As she shook the stars out of her eyes and struggled to compose herself, Steve presented her with a real diamond engagement ring.

She was even more surprised when she saw this, because they had never gone shopping together for a ring. Steve had gone to Christine's favorite jewelry store and enlisted the aid of her jeweler, who not only found out her ring size but also took note of what kinds of rings she liked. This clever jeweler had manipulated Christine into helping out a young man who happened to be in the store the same day as she, shopping for an engagement ring.

Christine was truly impressed and touched that Steve, who had never before been able to keep anything from her, managed to pull off the biggest, most romantic and original surprise of her life.

HOT TIP FOR SCUBA-SAVVY SUITORS: Be sure that the object of your affections not only is going to say yes, but is also an experienced, confident diver. Panic and fear can be a dangerous mix for divers.

a fine-feathered infatuation

Brent Arndt, an assistant manager at Sav-On Drug, wasn't too thrilled about driving an hour and fifteen minutes from St. Joseph, Michigan, to Valparaiso, Indiana, just to go to a nightclub. But he lost a coin flip with his two buddies, so off they went. Besides, there wasn't much to do in the small town of St. Joe's.

Lori, a toll-booth worker who lives in Valparaiso, had also ended up at the nightclub that night because she lost a coin toss with her girlfriends. She was tired of going to the same club all the time and seeing the same people, but when she spotted tall, handsome Brent across the room, she thought he was the most attractive guy she'd ever seen and started up a conversation with him. She didn't want to appear too forward, so she went back to talk to her girlfriends after only a brief chat. But this gave Brent the courage to ask her to dance a bit later. Although he thought she was geographically undesirable, Brent was taken with this attractive, straightforward woman. When he asked for her phone number, however, he wasn't sure she'd give him the right one. Lori admits that nine out of ten times, she usually gives out a fake number to avoid rejecting a man outright. But she liked Brent, so she gave him her real phone number, although she actually had little faith that a guy who lived more than an hour away from her would call.

Of course, he did call, and although their first date wasn't until two or three weeks after their very brief first meeting, sparks definitely flew, and they had a fantastic time. After that, they went out together every weekend. Lori would drive to St. Joe's, or Brent would make the journey to Valparaiso.

They dated for two and a half years before Brent got around to proposing, although Lori brought up the subject quite often about eighteen months into the relationship. She insists that she wasn't pushing the two of them toward the altar; she simply wanted reassurance that this was a serious, committed relationship. Brent wasn't against moving in the nuptial direction, he just wasn't quite ready yet.

The turning point for Brent was when his company relocated him to Jackson, Michigan. For the first time in his life, he lived far away from his family, and even farther away from Lori (a three-hour drive). He realized how much he missed her during this time, and decided he was ready to propose.

But how? Brent and Lori had already picked out an engagement ring, which Brent was to hold until he was ready to pop the question. Lori let him know that she wanted an actual proposal, and she wanted to be surprised. She wanted something unique, something she would always remember, and Brent decided to surpass her expectations. He's a somewhat conservative shirt-and-tie kind of guy, a businessman, not usually spontaneous, while Lori's the more artistic, creative, adventurous one of the pair. He's kind of shy, and she's outgoing. He wanted to be completely out of character when he proposed, and throw her a curve ball she never could have anticipated.

Slowly, a wacky idea began to form in his mind. Brent, who had been tall and skinny in adolescence, had earned the nickname "Big Bird" from his friends. Big Bird also brings to mind a chicken, which is how Brent characterizes himself during the period in which he was scared to make the big marriage commitment. And so, he decided to rent a Big Bird costume for a proposal that would truly express his lighter side. Brent went to visit his folks in St. Joe's and stopped at the town's costume shop. Lo and behold, there was a Big Bird costume on display right next to the cash register. This was truly a sign that his idea was meant to be.

Costume in hand, and that Wednesday, on body, Brent set out for Valparaiso. Lori was working at the Valparaiso toll booth and didn't know Brent had the day off. He was a bit worried that someone would call the state police on him, which is what toll booth employees are supposed to do if they see any suspicious characters in the vicinity, but he marshaled his courage and drove toward his destination in full Big Bird regalia. The temperature that day was ninety-eight degrees, but Brent was too nervous to notice. He had other reasons to sweat.

Brent stopped off in Valparaiso to pick up Lori's mother, whom he'd told earlier about the proposal. His nervousness was compounded when Lori's mother con-fessed that she'd alerted the local newspaper, which was excited about covering the event. They arrived at the toll station at the height of rush hour and parked far enough away from Lori's toll booth to make sure she wouldn't spot his car. He stepped out of the car and put on the Big Bird head (he's too tall—six-foot-five—to have worn it in the car). Now about seven feet tall, Big Bird began his 150-yard-long walk in sweltering heat toward Lori's toll booth. Rush-hour commuters honked and hooted at the giant *Sesame Street* character, and children cheered as he made his lumbering way toward his goal.

When Big Bird reached Lori's toll booth, she was shocked and had no idea that her boyfriend was inside the costume. Big Bird held up a large white poster-board card that asked, "Hi, are you Lori Sinar? Please check off one of the boxes." Although bewildered by this bizarre appari-tion, she managed to hold on to the blue marker that Big

Bird handed her and check off the "yes" box, her hands shaking. The giant yellow bird then presented her with another card that said, "Prove it—what's your badge number?" She wrote down her badge number on the card. Big Bird then showed her a third card that said, "A special friend of yours has sent me here to visit you, and I have something for you."

Big Bird then handed Lori a paper bag. Inside was a golden egg, which she took out of the bag, her hands shaking, as Big Bird showed her the fourth and final card. It said, "Hi, sweetie, will you marry me?" Lori started crying and looking around for Brent, but when Big Bird got on one knee, she realized with a shock that Big Bird *was* Brent. Big Bird then opened up the egg; inside was her engagement ring. She was overwhelmed, crying with surprise and happiness as the newspaper reporter snapped pictures and truckers shouted congratulations and feathers went up her nose as she hugged her fiancé. It was the happiest day of her life.

my temperature's rising

Sean directs IMAX films and commercials, and Shari is an "actuarial headhunter." Although their careers couldn't be more different, the two of them met by chance while waiting for tables in a restaurant. The more outgoing of the two, Shari introduced herself. She thought Sean was quite nice looking, despite the fact that he had a beard and mustache at the time, which definitely wasn't to her taste. They hit it off so well that the two decided to have lunch together in the restaurant. Sean was to leave town within a week for a brief assignment in Korea, so he didn't waste any time. He asked Shari to go to a museum with him four days later.

While they were at the museum, Shari was surprised to find herself overwhelmingly attracted to Sean. It was how he smelled, she says. He doesn't wear cologne, but his natural aroma was making it difficult for her to concentrate on the art treasures surrounding her. She was smitten.

About a month into their relationship, Sean handed Shari a pair of scissors and asked her if she'd like to cut off his beard and mustache. She was only too happy to comply, and as she suspected, Sean was even better looking with a clean-shaven face. This was only one of the many ways in which Sean devoted himself to pleasing his new love.

Early on, Shari let Sean know that she wasn't into wasting time with a partner who feared commitment. About two months into the relationship, she told him that if marriage and children weren't on his ultimate life agenda, he should let her know. Sean wasn't put off by her honesty and was willing to explore their relationship fully.

After about a year and a half, Shari moved in. Occasionally she would ask Sean what he was waiting for. She was ready for marriage, but he needed more time. Finally, she stopped asking (a major exercise in self-control for this outspoken woman), which gave Sean the space to get to the betrothal phase on his own.

When they had been living together about a year, Sean decided he was ready to take the big leap, but he wanted his proposal to be a surprise. He bought an inexpensive ring, a "stand-in ring," as he describes it, because he figured that Shari would want to have the chance to pick out her own real engagement ring. Then he formulated his plan.

Shari uses a natural method of birth control called the symptothermal method, which requires her to take her temperature upon waking every morning. As part of their daily morning ritual, Shari sleepily asks Sean to hand her the thermometer, which they keep on the nightstand next to his side of the bed. (Because of the shape of their bedroom, they can only put a nightstand on one side of the bed, and that's the side he likes to occupy.) At any rate, it keeps him involved in the process.

On this particular morning, however, which happened to be her birthday, Shari wondered in her half-asleep state why she was handed a small velvet box instead of her thermometer. She quickly recovered from her confusion and surprise, and was overcome with joy. Sean just smiled and said, "Happy Birthday." About ten minutes later, now fully awake, Shari realized that Sean hadn't actually asked her to marry him, and reminded him of this omission. He said those four magic words, and her coy response was, "I'll have to think about it." Sean and Shari shared a laugh about this, but a few hours later, Sean became a bit concerned. "Don't worry," she reassured him, "of course I'll marry you."

a not-so-perfectly programmed proposal

When Josie and Jim met, they were merely office acquaintances at the same company. She was a secretary and he was a caterer in the company's executive dining room. Their first "date" was when they attended traffic school together, but their relationship didn't really take off until they went to Europe together. Jim had won two round-trip tickets to Europe through a contest he'd entered on a whim, and since he didn't have any spending money for the trip (nor anyone special to take with him), he put up a company bulletin board notice offering to sell one of the tickets. Josie offered to buy the ticket, since she was interested in visiting a friend who lived in Germany. Because one of the conditions of the prize was that both tickets be used at the same time and for the same destinations, these two casual acquaintances began the unusual task of planning a transatlantic trip together.

As they began making their travel plans, the two realized they were attracted to each other, although Jim was a bit gun-shy after the breakup of his last relationship. He was also a bit shy in general. But when the more gregarious Josie took the initiative and made her move at the office Christmas party, Jim didn't hesitate. This made their impending trip even more exciting, and the romance quickly bloomed as the new couple began getting to know each other as well as various European cities. Josie has one particularly fond memory of spending her birthday at a wonderful Parisian restaurant with Jim, who from time to time would scribble in a notebook. Consequently, the French waiters assumed he was an American food critic, and the service and cuisine were beyond compare.

The only down side of their trip to Europe was the fact that they both lost their jobs when they came back. The company had consented to give them just two weeks of vacation time, but Jim and Josie had insisted that they had to have a full month, offering to take the other two weeks without pay. They had known there was a risk, and they took it—and never regretted it. Josie's now a court reporter, and Jim is a musician.

Their engagement didn't happen until four years later, although the pair began living together not long after their return to the United States. Josie started throwing out hints about marriage, and although Jim didn't protest, he didn't say much of anything about the subject. He wasn't quite ready just yet for a proposal. He mulled the matter over quietly for months, waiting for the moment when he had the right rush of emotions, the moment when he would just know it was right for him to take the leap.

Then one night while a guest was over for dinner, Jim had his "moment." Suddenly he was struck with the knowledge and the certainty that he needed to marry Josie, and he knew he had to act immediately, or else he might start procrastinating again. A plan quickly took shape in his mind. He excused himself and went into the bedroom to turn on the computer, in which he had recently installed a sound card. Jim recorded a message to Josie, which would be playing when she retired for the evening, and which he programmed to play endlessly. The message said, in Jim's voice: "Look at the book, *The Prophet*. Page 15. I love you." This page from Khalil Gibran's famous book was about marriage, with verses that had been used in his sister's wedding vows, and he knew Josie would get the idea. Jim's proposal method was romantic, it was unique, and he returned to the dining room with a mingled sense of relief and anticipation, hardly able to wait until Josie went to bed and heard his computerized message of eternal love.

Unfortunately, Jim's plans went awry. Not exactly a night person, Josie was so sleepy by the time she went to bed that she heard the message, but it didn't register. Annoyed by the sound, she turned to Jim and asked, "How do you turn that damn thing off?" Not exactly what he had envisioned when Cupid struck him with a betrothal arrow. A bit crushed, Jim complied and turned off the computer.

To make matters worse, Josie was in a bad mood the next morning and demanded to know what he was doing on the computer the night before. Jim was miffed and wasn't about to tell her. He decided to say nothing about it and concluded that either she'd eventually figure out the message, or she wouldn't. Relations between the two were a bit strained for about a week, until Josie brought up the computer message once again. "What were you trying to do with the computer?" she pressed. When she first heard the message in her half-asleep state, she couldn't believe that Jim was actually proposing, because she had brought up the subject of marriage months before and he'd never responded. She'd long assumed that Jim just wasn't taking the whole marriage idea seriously. But after thinking about that message for a week, she finally said, "Were you proposing?" Exasperated, Jim replied, "What did you think I was doing?"

The mystery solved, the two laughed about it, and Josie of course said yes. She still loves to play Jim's message over and over on the computer.

dramas great and small

life's too short to wait

Martha Cronin and Glenn Lambert had been living together for about seven years. Although they were undoubtedly committed to their relationship, marriage was always an abstract possibility, something neither of them ever seemed to be ready for. Both had the erratic incomes of freelancers: Martha worked in film production; Glenn in radio. They always figured that someday, when they were making money more regularly, when everything was perfect, well, then they might consider getting married and starting a family. There was plenty of time for all that.

When Martha found herself on location with a film in Santa Fe, Glenn took the opportunity to combine a visit to his beloved with his lifelong desire to see the city where his parents told him he'd been conceived. The peaceful, ethereal beauty of Santa Fe lived up to Glenn's expectations. He and Martha decided to invite Glenn's parents to fly in from New York and take a nostalgic look at the place where they'd spent two of the happiest years of their early married life.

At dinner one night in a restaurant where Glenn's parents fondly remembered dining back in the 1940s, his father, Dr. Bruno Lambert, was swept up in the nostalgia of his surroundings. To Glenn's surprise, his father began talking about his experiences during World War II, a subject that, for Glenn, had always been taboo in his family. Glenn knew that his parents, German Jews, had escaped from Germany in 1938, and that his grandparents had died there. He'd heard stories of how his mother, Margaret, born Gretel Bergmann, had trained as a high jumper for the 1936 Berlin Olympics, but had been banned from participating in the games because she was a Jew. He also knew that his father had returned to Germany as an American soldier to fight the Nazis, but any details beyond those broad facts had always been far too sensitive an issue to be disclosed.

Bruno talked of how he enlisted in the U.S. Army on the very same day he got his citizenship papers. He was shipped off to the front lines in Europe, with the joyful knowledge that he and his wife were expecting their first child. The thought of a baby on the way comforted him immeasurably and got him through the hardships of soldiering. From the battlefields of France all the way to Germany, he wrote his wife every day, love letters in which he expressed his hopes and dreams for their child-to-be, whom he'd already decided would be named Joseph. What he didn't know was that his wife had already lost the baby. She wrote him with the sad news, but her letter took many months to reach him. In the meantime, she continued to receive his heartbreaking letters in which he rejoiced over their child who was not to be. When Bruno came back from the war, he was stationed in Santa Fe, and there, Glenn was conceived.

Glenn's father also told Glenn and Martha, for the very first time, about how he had managed to reach the United States, and, once there, how he tried to get his parents out of Nazi Germany. He tried borrowing money, obtaining a sponsor for them to come to this country, all in vain. After all his attempts to save them, Bruno's parents were murdered in Auschwitz.

Glenn and Martha listened with rapt attention to Bruno's stories, and when they went back to their hotel room that night, they felt as if they'd been emotionally transformed. They could only imagine what it must have been like to live through such pain and heartbreak and felt nothing but admiration for Glenn's parents. With the world falling apart all around them, having left their family and possessions behind in a country ravaged by hatred and genocide, Glenn's parents had wholeheartedly embraced the idea of committing their lives to each other and bringing a child into the world.

Glenn and Martha sat up practically all night, talking of their love for each other, and weeping with both joy and sadness over what they had learned from Glenn's father. They decided that every moment is a precious gift, and that they should no longer wait for some faraway perfect set of circumstances that would make marriage seem like the right thing to do. They decided to get married and have children, and announced their happy news to Glenn's parents the next morning at breakfast.

crime and courtship

David had been seeing Christina for three and a half years. She'd made it clear for some time that she wanted to get married, but David wasn't ready yet. After the two survived the Los Angeles earthquake of 1994 and moved back to the calmer shores of Washington, D.C., David found an exciting job as a video and commercial producer for the Washington Bullets. Now that he was set up in a promising career and Christina had secured a position as a kindergarten teacher, David decided he was ready to get engaged. He wanted to infuse a bit of drama into his proposal, however.

As a Christmas treat, David took Christina to see *Tommy* at the Kennedy Center. After the show, they were in high spirits as they headed toward the parking lot. As they arrived at the empty space where they'd parked David's prized Isuzu Rodeo, they realized that David's car had been stolen. David was in a panic, practically in tears. Christina was also upset, and a little ashamed to admit to herself that the first thing that went through her mind was that David might not be able to afford a ring now. She tried her best to calm him, but both were terribly shaken.

As they walked back toward the Kennedy Center to

use the phone, David and Christina argued over whom they should call first, their roommate or the police. They passed a parked limousine, and David suggested they ask the driver whether he'd seen anything that looked like a car theft in the parking lot. Christina was annoyed by this suggestion, preferring to call the police rather than waste time bothering a perfect stranger, but David insisted. The driver, to Christina's puzzlement, immediately stepped out and solicitously opened the limo door for David, who coaxed Christina inside. What happened next was not an inquiry into the whereabouts of David's car. Instead, David got down on one knee to make a proposal of marriage, complete with a beautiful engagement ring. Christina happily accepted, but what about the car?

David admitted that he'd secretly arranged with his sister to pick up the car while they were at the show, and had, of course, also hired the limousine. His former training as an actor came in handy, for he had been most convincing in his anguish over the missing car. He'd achieved the dramatic effect he wanted, to transport Christina from the depths of despair to the heights of unexpected joy. Sound cruel? Well, it happens to audiences all the time

during the climactic scenes of the best films, as David had learned while critiquing scripts in Los Angeles.

Christina was too delighted to hold David's theatrics against him, and the blissful lovers spent the next couple of hours riding around D.C. in the back of a limo, taking in the fairy-tale beauty of the capital decked out in all its Christmas splendor, drinking champagne, and calling their friends with their happy news.

pull (the wool) over, lady

Angelo's diner is right across the street from the police station, so it's no wonder that it's a regular hangout for those in law enforcement.

Allison has been serving up breakfast on the 5 A.M. shift of this small-town eatery since high school. John, a policeman, was often her first customer. He immediately took a fancy to the charming young woman. She thought he was a real nice guy, but he was a twenty-six-year-old man of the world, and she was only eighteen. Whoever got Allison would be a lucky guy, he thought, but, he sighed, he would have to set his sights elsewhere, and he did. Allison and John would remain just friends. He would bring in pictures of his dog and tell her his problems, and she would tell her mother about the handsome police officer who asked her for advice.

One day, John confided in Allison that he wanted to propose to the woman he was dating. Did Allison think that his girlfriend would like him to surprise her with the ring or allow her to pick it out with him? Thinking this question was so typically considerate of this lovely man, Allison thought about how she'd love to be lucky enough to have someone as wonderful as John propose to her. She answered that she would be happy to have a ring but also happy to pick it out. Well, John did marry his girlfriend, but his marriage lasted only six months. His wife left him for an old boyfriend, and John took the breakup hard. He was determined to stay out of circulation, but his friends knew that he felt close to Allison and encouraged him to ask her out. John thought about it long and hard. She was now twenty-two. All right, he thought, he'd do it.

Allison was surprised by the invitation. It was awkward for both of them because they'd already known each other for four years and neither had had the nerve to indicate their interest in the other. John says the fact that they're together was meant to be, because there was plenty more to prevent them from ever connecting romantically: the age difference, his marriage and divorce, and her plan to finish college and move to England to stay with her aunt. Any one of these things might have split them apart, but instead they ended up together.

Once they started dating, they quickly became an item. Together they did exciting new things: canoeing, a rodeo, bike riding, Broadway shows, and two Elton John concerts. And they were always playing practical jokes on each other. One day Allison was at John's apartment, and they were looking at John's old photographs. She quietly pocketed an old Polaroid of him when he was twelve years old. In the picture, John was wearing jeans and no shirt and posing like a muscle man.

She gave the photo to their mutual friend, a sergeant also named John who used to come into the diner with

John. Allison thought the sergeant would embarrass John by tacking up the photo on the bulletin board, but he did much better than that. He blew it up to an eleven-by-fourteen print and made a bunch of copies. On each one he inserted a funny caption. Then he tacked them up all over the precinct: in the cells, in the hallway, on the windows—everywhere. When John saw this, he drove straight over to the diner and announced that Allison had met her match.

He prepared a cardboard-backed, professional-looking beauty pageant poster. It said, "Allison King, Miss Garrison Lake 1995, First Place." On the poster were icons of horseshoes and a large crown. He left this on the back of Allison's jeep. People started coming into the diner and congratulating Allison. After the third well-wisher, Allison looked out of the diner window and saw the big sign on her vehicle. She ran out and ripped it off.

Both were good sports and were having the time of their lives together. After four months of dating, they began to talk about families. She loves children and always wanted to start a family early in life, so she could grow up with her kids. He always wanted children as well.

John remembers that when they talked about getting engaged, she'd get very excited and her face would light up. He'd get a big kick out of that. He wanted her to like the engagement ring, and so he allowed her to come with him to choose it, although she had no idea when she was going to get it.

He began brainstorming a special way of proposing— one that would be as unique as their relationship, and one that would combine the playful elements of their courtship. And he hit upon just the thing. He decided to relate the proposal to their jobs, which, after all, is where it all began.

On February 24, 1996, Allison was driving to work as usual at 4:45 A.M. As she drove her jeep past the intersection of Main and Union, she heard a siren and saw the flashing light of a police car in her rearview mirror. She pulled over, and a policeman she had never seen before walked over to her. His name was Barry. He said to Allison, "Your taillight is out; would you please step out of the vehicle so I can show you." Allison was scared. She didn't know Barry and didn't know how to respond. He repeated the demand.

As Allison stepped out of the jeep, two cops named Lou and Ed drove up in their police cars with their emergency lights flashing. They aimed blinding spotlights on Allison's little jeep, so she couldn't see right away that Ed was holding a video camera. Allison was relieved to see at least one police officer, Lou, that she did recognize. At once she asked nervously if Lou knew where John was. She didn't have to wait long for an answer. A few moments later, John appeared, sneaking up in his own police car.

When she saw John she smiled and said, "What's going on?" He had the ring box in his hand and acted as if this was a regular police incident. "What did you do now?" he asked Allison. "Why are they stopping you?"

John told Barry not to cut Allison any breaks, that he should do what he had to do. Then John went up to her and got down on one knee, opened up the box, and asked her to marry him. Her exact words were "Yes, of course."

As they hugged, her hands were shaking and her eyes were tearing up. Everyone was watching, and she realized then that the entire scene was being videotaped by Ed.

She and John were both nervous. John began to put the ring on the wrong hand. It took a while, but he found her left hand, slipped the ring on it, and sent her off to work with a kiss. Then, as she had done almost every morning for several years, Allison drove past the police station and turned into the parking lot of Angelo's diner.

absence makes the heart grow fonder

Jen, now managing director of the Drama League in New York, was a theater and television actor when she met Matt, who is now an attorney and aspiring screenwriter. They met when Jen and her roommate secured part-time jobs for themselves at the Metropolitan Museum. She was immediately attracted to Matt, a handsome young man she spotted working at one of the cash registers, and before she introduced herself, he was referred to by her and her roommate as "Register Number Two."

Jen was an outgoing sort, and quickly started working on Matt to go out with her, but her hints were too subtle for the shy Matt, who needed to be hit over the head to realize a charming, beautiful woman like Jen could be interested in him. His mother even pointed Jen out one day when she was visiting the museum as a woman he should ask for a date. Finally, Jen got through to Matt, they started dating, and before long they became serious.

After about eighteen months, Jen got a job offer to go to London for a year. Matt had decided to shelve his filmmaking dreams for the time being, and was planning on starting law school in Boston in a matter of months.

Neither of them had even thought about marriage, let alone discussed it, but their imminent separation began to weigh heavily upon Matt, who silently mulled over the fate of their relationship. They had a wonderful thing going. How would a year apart affect them?

Slowly the idea of proposing formed in his mind, and he went out and bought a very untraditional ring shaped like a G clef and set with a sapphire. But even with the ring, he lacked the courage to propose, and held onto it for months. The date of their imminent separation loomed ever closer.

After what seemed an eternity of procrastination, Matt surprised himself by marshaling his courage one morning as he and Jen were lying in bed together. Very tentatively, Matt said, "Jen . . . would you maybe, kinda, sorta consider getting married—someday?" Jen answered, "Uh-huh," thinking that this was not a proposal, but rather an opening of a discussion of a possible future. Noting her puzzled expression when he did not continue in this vein, Matt said, "Well, uh . . . I have a ring." At this point, Jen realized he was serious, and, surprised but quite pleased, she blurted out, "Yes!" Matt then told her he didn't have the ring with him, and added that it was "different," and he hoped she'd like it. Despite her joy over their unexpected engagement, Jen inwardly dreaded being presented with the ring, since Matt's and her respective tastes in clothes and jewelry were invariably at opposite ends of the fashion spectrum. To her amazement, she was thrilled with this unusual engagement ring, and realized she couldn't have made a better choice if she had picked it out herself.

Jen did spend her year in England, and Matt went off to school in Boston, but by traveling as couriers, they managed to visit each other six times during their long separation. That year of surviving a long-distance relationship was a tremendous challenge for both of them, but they realize now that they might not have made as great an effort to stay in touch and visit, may have even drifted apart in some respects, had they not gotten engaged beforehand. Having made that formal declaration of their love, they managed to make their separation the glue that cemented their relationship together. Now they are rarely apart for more than a couple of days, and cherish the precious pleasures of living together.

airborne amour

mystery lovers

When Robbert, a banking officer, decided to propose to Linda, he faced a most difficult challenge. Both lovers of mysteries, Robbert and Linda delighted in unraveling the most convoluted and unusual plots of the movies they enjoyed. The couple had discussed marriage and knew it was what they wanted, but Linda let it be known that not only did she want a formal proposal and a ring, she wanted the proposal to be a surprise. Pulling the wool over Linda's amateur detective's eyes would certainly be a daunting task, but one that Robbert took up with determination and ingenuity.

Linda and Robbert lived in different cities, and after Linda finished working at a computer trade show in Robbert's town, she planned on spending the weekend there with Robbert. But instead of driving her back to his place after the trade show, Robbert drove to the airport, announcing that he was taking her to San Francisco. Linda's detective radar was immediately activated, and she felt certain that Robbert intended to take her to San Francisco to propose.

As they toured around the jeweled city by the bay, taking in the various sights, Linda quietly waited for Robbert to spring his "surprise." At a romantic dinner that first night, Robbert told her how much he loved her, and handed her a beautifully wrapped box, which he said was a symbol of his love. This must be it, she thought, as she confidently tore off the paper and ribbons. But to her surprise (and disappointment), the box contained not a ring but a perfumed candle. Linda kept her emotions to herself and thanked Robbert for the gift.

The next night, they dined at the Cliff House, a famous restaurant with an ocean view. As they sat by the fireplace, soft music playing in the background, Robbert handed her another prettily wrapped box. This is definitely it, thought Linda. Robbert then told her that the box contained all of the unknown mysteries and adventures they would share, all the love and romance they already shared, and all the trust—the trust that she would never open this box. Taken aback, Linda asked if she'd heard correctly. Did Robbert really mean that she couldn't open the box? Yes, Robbert said with a smile, she couldn't open it because it represented the unknown in their relationship, the mystery that would always keep their romance alive.

Next, Robbert suggested they take a walk on the beach before leaving for the airport to go back home. Linda thought to herself that perhaps Robbert didn't want to propose in a public place like a restaurant, that perhaps he would ask for her hand on the beach, a more secluded setting. But no proposal came, and as they drove off for the airport, with barely enough time to make their plane, Linda became agitated. She said nothing about her disappointment, but Robbert noticed her anxiety and soothingly assured her that they would make their flight in plenty of time. Missing the flight wasn't what was on her mind, of course, but Robbert seemed blissfully unaware of this fact. Linda couldn't get over her disappointment. Knowing Robbert's awareness of her suspicious mind, she expected him to pull a diversion or two to throw her off, but she had been sure that a proposal would occur by the end of their weekend in San Francisco. There was no explanation for it other than Robbert was pulling a cruel joke on her, and that hurt. If this was an elaborate game of cat-and-mouse, Linda failed to find the humor in it. She couldn't let him know, because she didn't want to seem ungrateful for the otherwise beautiful weekend he'd given her.

They did indeed miss their flight, which made Linda even more upset, because at this point she was so disappointed that all she wanted to do was to go home. Robbert got them on another flight, a packed Southwest Airlines plane. During the trip, Robbert left his seat to use the bathroom, and a few minutes later, a flight attendant announced over the plane's loudspeaker that Linda was to come to the front of the plane. Shocked and confused, and arousing the curiosity of the other passengers, Linda left her seat at the back of the plane and arrived at the front section of the plane, where a smiling flight attendant was waiting.

To her surprise, Robbert stepped out from behind a partition and got on his knees in the aisle, holding the intercom microphone. He took Linda's hand in his, and with a trembling voice declared his love, for all the passengers on board to hear, and asked her to be his wife. The passengers cheered and clapped wildly. Linda could not have been more caught off guard. Overcome by emotion, she knelt beside Robbert, who embraced her and slipped a ring on her finger. She said yes, of course, but Robbert was too nervous to hand her the microphone.

As they walked that long, long aisle back to their seats, faces tear-streaked but beaming, the passengers were swept up in the couple's euphoria, cheering, offering congratulations, handshakes, and best wishes. The Southwest flight attendants congratulated Linda and Robbert more than once over the loudspeaker and served the newly engaged couple champagne.

Robbert could not have asked for a greater success in outsmarting his supersleuth sweetheart. He knew her suspicions would be aroused by their unexpected trip to San Francisco, a place where he'd never gone and a city they'd always talked about someday visiting together. He knew she'd expect a proposal there, and that the only way to ensure a surprise was to not propose to her there. Although it was hard for him to see his love so disappointed as they left San Francisco, he knew that she'd forgive him once he proposed in the air.

HOT TIP FOR PROPOSING IN THE SKY: Robbert called the airline in advance to find out if its policy would allow him to pull off his proposal. While Southwest was more than happy to comply, it's a good idea to call the airline and find out what specific arrangements need to be made in advance. Policies vary, and some airlines won't allow passengers to commandeer the loudspeaker.

on italian soil

Christina and Kevin had been living together for two years in a house they'd bought together, and although they had agreed that they would eventually tie the knot officially, Kevin always shied away from making any real plans in that direction. Outspoken, fiery, and a lightning-quick decision maker, Christina let Kevin know on several occasions that she was ready for marriage. Kevin, on the other hand, was shy and quietly pragmatic, taking action at his own pace, a pace which was often a challenge for Christina.

When Christina learned that her dream of writing a travel book on northern Italy was to come true, she and Kevin made plans to take an extended trip there. Christina took the opportunity to broach the marriage subject again by telling all their friends and family (in front of Kevin, of course) that Kevin was going to propose to her in Italy. After all, it was the most romantic setting on the planet and would be the perfect place for him to propose. Christina's plan became a joke between them, but she knew in her heart it was serious business. When she overheard Kevin telling friends about it on the phone, she assumed that it would indeed happen as she hoped.

Very early in their relationship, Christina and Kevin had

taken an Italian holiday together, and she remembered Italy, particularly Venice, as the place where they'd fallen in love. Italy was indeed as romantic as she and Kevin remembered; however, on this book-writing trip, the pressures of moving from town to town and gathering the material Christina needed to complete her book exhausted both of them. Christina thought for sure Kevin would propose in Venice, but their days there ended uneventfully. Nevertheless, Christina kept thinking that each new place they explored, and each romantic city they remembered from their earlier trip would be the place where Kevin would ask her to marry him. Her disappointment grew as they left each city, still without a proposal, but she kept her hurt feelings to herself. She'd hinted enough, made it quite clear that she wanted marriage, and she wanted Kevin to take the initiative and ask her. Aside from her desire for a traditional proposal from the man she loved, it was the only way she could be sure he was truly ready and wanted to marry her as much as she wanted to marry him.

The last night of their trip they were in Rome, and Christina burst into tears, finally asking Kevin why he hadn't proposed. He felt terrible when he realized how disappointed she was, and said that with all the frantic running around, it had never seemed like the right time. He assured her that he loved her, and she took some comfort in his words. Although he made an attempt to propose right then and there, she stopped him. They were both too emotionally upset, and that wasn't the way she wanted to be asked. There's still time, she thought. We're still in Italy.

The next day they boarded their plane in Rome, a bit sad to be leaving Italy, but taking pleasure in reminiscing about all the wonderful experiences they'd shared. As they fastened their seatbelts and the plane prepared to take off, Christina took Kevin's hand and reminded him they were still on Italian soil. She asked if there were something he wanted to say to her. At this point, the airplane was taxiing down the runway, building up speed. As the force of the engines pinned them back against their seats and the front wheels began to lift off the ground, Kevin turned to Christina and asked her to marry him. She said yes, and the plane took off.

flight 159, i love you

In September 1993, Amy and Larry were planning a trip to Florida, but Larry had something more in mind. Having "nothing better to do that day," he thought this might just be a good opportunity to propose, and set his mind to finding a way to do so with a splash. Larry doesn't like to do anything in a low-key way—he'll tell you himself he's a loud and showy person.

His first thought was to make a video and show it on the plane. However, when he contacted the customer service department at TWA to find out what kind of video equipment the airline used, he learned there was to be no movie on their flight. So he had to scratch that idea.

Undeterred, Larry conceived a new plan. He inquired about making an announcement on the plane, but no, TWA wouldn't let him do that, either; it would not be courteous to other passengers who sometimes fly because, for example, there is a death in the family.

OK, OK, he would just have to propose on the plane

without the loudspeaker. That was fine with TWA. The customer service person called the flight crew to let them know that Larry intended to propose on the plane.

Larry arrived at La Guardia airport one hour before he was to meet Amy there for TWA's Flight 159 to sunny Florida. Ring in hand (engraved "flight 159 I love you"), Larry checked in with the ticket counter woman who already was informed of Larry's plan. And just as in the movies where the small-town justice of the peace also runs the post office and the grocery store, it turned out the ticket counter woman was also the woman at the gate.

He gave her flowers to stow away on the plane for him, and she alerted the flight crew. This helpful woman also arranged for Larry to walk through security a few times to make sure the ring wouldn't set the buzzer off. Then Larry went back outside to meet Amy at curbside where they were to check their luggage. The baggage checker patted Larry on the back. It seemed the whole airport was in on the conspiracy.

Together they boarded the plane. Walking behind Amy, Larry clandestinely made eye contact with Phil, the flight attendant, and they both knew what was going to happen next.

Two minutes into the flight, Larry told Amy he was going to get some water. He located coconspirator Phil and began to discuss his plan to propose. Phil suggested, "Why don't you make an announcement?" When Larry explained that he was told he could not, Phil replied, bless his heart, "You can do anything you want; this is my flight!"

Then Phil asked Larry when he might want to do this, and Larry said, "Well, I thought after you served your food and beverage." But take-charge Phil replied, "Why don't you just do it now?"

"Yikes," Larry thought, "there is no turning back now." He went back to sit with Amy for a few moments and compose himself, but he was nervous and panicky. Amy asked what was wrong, and he fibbed, "Nothing." To throw her off track, Larry then proclaimed, "I know a lot of people are thinking we'll be getting engaged this weekend, but we're not; it's not going to happen." He pleaded poverty as his excuse, and this much was true. He had spent his whole life savings on a lovely ring.

Amy was looking at her hand, because her usually well polished nails were in bad shape. Using this as inspiration, Larry added, "Besides, I couldn't ask you with those nails." Unfazed, she responded, pointing to her ring finger, "That one still looks good."

Five minutes later, Larry told Amy he would be back in a few minutes.

"Where are you going?" she asked.

"To get a deck of cards."

"Why don't you have them bring it?" she insisted.

"No, I don't want to bother them," he countered.

She wasn't buying this line, which was so uncharacteristic of Larry.

"But that's their job," she said.

Finally, Larry just gave her a weak smile and left his seat.

Seconds later flight attendant Phil's voice came over the loudspeaker: "We have a passenger who would like to make an announcement. Would the person sitting in row 17E please press the flight attendant's lighted button."

"Oh, boy," Amy thought, "That's me!" With all eyes glued on her, Amy looked up the aisle and saw Larry standing there. Before she knew it, Larry took the microphone and proudly announced, "This is for the girl in row 17 whom I've been with for four years. I love her very much, and I want everyone on the plane to know how much I love her. She's very special and has made me completely happy over the last four years. Now I'm going to go back there and ask Amy to marry me."

And that's what he did. He marched right back there and got on his knees and asked her in front of a whole planeload of people. All of the Florida senior citizens were gushing and applauding, people were high-fiving Larry, the flight attendant brought Amy the roses, and the Florida grandmothers were asking her, "So, honey, are you going to say yes?"

Amy started to cry and finally said yes through the tears, after which they were moved up to first class and given a bag full of little bottles of liquor and champagne. And contrary to what TWA customer service may have thought, no one on the plane seems to have minded at all.

if music be the food of love, rock on

love is the pits

Both fortysomething, Marcia and Bill met in cyber-space in November 1994, while trading e-mails on America Online. Marcia, a Rutgers University professor, lived with her teenage daughters in a two-family house in Highland Park, New Jersey. Bill, a banker, lived an hour and a half away in Westchester County, New York. By the time they met face-to-face in January of 1995, they were still strangers, but it was to be only five months more until they were married . . .

It was not unusual that a banker and an English profes-sor should share an interest in music. Like many people their age, they liked both Bach and Zappa, but unlike many of their contemporaries, they found they shared a particular fondness for loud rock and roll. Nothing gives Marcia more pleasure than cranking up the speakers and relaxing to the lilting sounds of heavy metal music, or even more precisely, death metal, speed metal, and thrash. Until Bill met Marcia, he preferred the quieter sounds of Nirvana and Pearl Jam. But she changed all that.

They had first found each other in the "romance connection" on America On Line and e-mailed each other every day. Mostly they wrote about rock music, exchanging musical lyrics and discussing them.

They e-mailed back and forth on their computers for about six weeks before ever talking on the phone. It turns out they both had children, and in their letters they also spoke about being parents. Marcia would compose long, beautiful, well-written letters, and Bill would write back brief letters, jokes, and promises to write more, but he actually wrote only one letter of substance. If it weren't for the rock-and-roll connection, she might have given up, because she couldn't tell if Bill was a serious person behind all the comedy.

What Bill found particularly attractive in Marcia's letters were the contrasts and ironies in her personality. She liked heavy metal but was also remarkably literate and appreciated James, Lawrence, and Freud. She was filled with heady ideas that Bill loved to hear.

Marcia's a little older than Bill, but as a body builder, she's in better shape. In so many ways she showed him that she had a lot of depth and character; this was not just another person on the other side of the keyboard. Bill, ever hiding behind his joker persona, got a better sense of

Marcia than she did of him. Nonetheless, they decided to meet, if only to determine if they wished to see more of each other.

They met under the train schedule board at Manhattan's Penn Station. Marcia was standing there with a backpack, and he walked up to her in his "banker uniform," his Sony Walkman headphones firmly in place. He would be "the geek in the suit but with a Walkman on," he had told her. Marcia had closely cropped hair with a long salt-and-pepper forelock jutting out from her forehead. Bill was expecting this. In his words: "I knew this, and still I went." And he adds, "She would be easy to pick out of a crowd in a football stadium."

Marcia was nervous about their meeting. What was this guy really going to be like? She didn't even know his last name. When he showed up with a twinkle in his eye and boyish good looks, she could just tell that he wasn't the usual rat in the rat race—one of the legions of indistinguishable men running to the train in a suit and raincoat. She says he was a "unique rat, a rat impersonator, actually; a rat wannabe."

The two went out for dinner to get better acquainted. They couldn't say there was instant chemistry between them; they didn't feel close yet. There wasn't great intimacy in their letters or even in this first meeting. Still, there was curiosity, although they're both fairly skeptical people. At dinner, conversation flowed. When Marcia asked for Bill's last name, which is unusual, Bill was surprised that Marcia spelled it correctly. Quite amazingly, it just so happened that Bill's cousin with the same last name is the other tenant in Marcia's two-family house.

As they approached the train station to say good-bye,

they decided that they did want to see more of each other and kissed goodnight. Hurried as it was, it was a great kiss that made them feel connected. "We meshed," they say in unison. "Something happened," Marcia reveals. "Something passed from mouth to mouth in addition to the saliva." She went home in a daze on the train. She "heard little birds flying around and chirping in her head." That was a Tuesday night.

They spoke on the phone the next day, and although they were "geographically challenged," they made a date for the following weekend. Manhattan had been neutral territory. Now he wanted her to come to Westchester. Marcia made the pilgrimage that Friday night, and they sat in front of the fireplace listening to the music of Pantera (panther in Spanish). Pantera specializes in speed metal, her favorite. Bill remembers Marcia banging her head back and forth in a very cute manner with her ponytail forelock swaying to and fro. She was wearing her Nine Inch Nails T-shirt (his favorite band), black jeans, and motorcycle boots with spikes. Bill had on jeans and a T-shirt. He saves the banker uniform for when he's "in service." Bill's hair is short, albeit a tad long for a banker.

The lights were low, the atmosphere romantic. Marcia had hoped to seduce Bill, and sparks did indeed fly. It was a glorious evening, and night, and morning—in all respects. This was the initial stage of love.

The relationship accelerated at lightning speed. Both agreed it was incredibly corny to say how much they were made for each other, but they couldn't help but admit they "were experiencing the reality of clichés." Within a month, Bill moved in.

Two weeks after they met—to some, that would be

very soon, but to them, it was an eternity—Marcia sent an e-mail signed "love." Bill said he couldn't utter the "L" word until he saw her; and the next time they got together, that's exactly what he did.

Very soon thereafter he started using the "M" word. Everything seemed to happen in alphabetical order: kiss, love, marriage. This was definitely getting serious.

Two months after they met, they went to a Pantera show at the Nassau Coliseum on Long Island. By now Bill was a true fan of this music, but this band attracts a particularly ugly crowd. Bill and Marcia were standing in the "mosh pit," a big open space with no seats, surrounded by masses of a certain form of human life they describe as "flying skinheads and Nazi dirtbags" (both Bill and Marcia are Jewish and particularly fond of this imagery).

Despite the band's Neanderthal following, Bill and Marcia agree that Pantera is "a very talented, powerful band, very musically creative and interesting." The pit where they stood was a typically chaotic swirl of bodies, sweat, other bodily fluids, skinheads, and Doc Marten boots.

Inevitably, there are always a few injuries at a so-called mosh scene. When asked, "Does this concern you?" Bill says "Yes." Marcia says "No." (Marcia, after all, is the body builder of the pair.) At the Pantera concert, they did protect their ears with earplugs. Still, Bill was wearing glasses and was not happy to realize he was the only one.

They were getting swirled and churned around with buckets of sweat when Pantera came on stage with a particularly romantic ballad entitled "Fucking Hostile." Oblivious to the flying skinheads, Bill watched his lady. Once more he was swept away by the way her hair banged around, and suddenly he was struck with the urgency of wanting to say something to her, to tell her how he felt about her.

He knew he simply couldn't live without her, and as the song wound down he reached over to pull out her earplugs and he was nervous and his hand was shaking and two-hundred-pound guys were hitting him in the back, and she helped him remove the earplugs, and he screamed at her "I love you," and she said "I love you, too," and he said "No, I really love you. Will you marry me?" and she said "What?" He screamed, "Will you marry me and be with me forever and be my wife?" but he just saw her mouth a response, and he repeated his request and finally he heard her say the magic word, "Yes."

With that, the song segued from "Fucking Hostile" to "This Love," which may sound romantic but is actually about a very twisted love affair. The singer expresses the wish to kill himself and his love because he had lied to himself when he said he loved her: "*I said I loved, but I lied.*"

They embraced to "This Love," and Bill felt he was in a situation where the innocent are protected. They were oblivious to the carnage around them and didn't get killed. They were getting hit, but it didn't hurt. Usually one takes a defensive posture in such an environment, but they were newly engaged. No one could have heard Bill's proposal, but the crowd control guy who sprays the crowd with water (into their mouths and on their heads to cool them off) kept squirting them, more than is customary, and they continued to embrace and kiss.

On June 6, Marcia and Bill exchanged vows in the mayor's office with wedding bands fashioned with little skulls. Although there was no music at their wedding, every day music fills their home. They attend lots of rock shows and cultural events. In one week they might see Shakespeare on Broadway, Fear Factory, and a concert at Lincoln Center. Surely, this is a match made in heaven.

will you (pretend to) marry me?

Tom is now a successful musician, composer, Internet publisher, and creator of "cyber cafés" on the Worldwide Web. But about fourteen years ago, Tom was a nineteen-year-old longing for a complete change in his life, which included breaking into the music business. He moved from his lovely English seaside hometown of Devon to the complete aesthetic opposite: the eternally gray, drab industrial city of Manchester. There, he landed a great job as lighting designer and production manager at a new rock club where all his favorite bands played. But the turn his life took was a bit more than he'd bargained for.

It all started one night at work, when Tom overheard Octavia, the pretty, twenty-six-year-old manager of the club's three bars, complaining to another coworker about one of the DJs. It seems this DJ was determined to seduce Octavia, but she was completely disinterested, and her suitor firmly refused to take no for an answer. At the time, Tom and this particular DJ hated each other, although in the years since then, the two have become friends. Tom thought the DJ was a real arrogant, sexist type and saw his opportunity through Octavia's dilemma to really push this guy's macho buttons. Although Tom and Octavia were complete strangers, had never even spoken to each other in this extremely large club, Tom walked up to Octavia and suggested that she tell the DJ that she and Tom were dating. Not only would this get the DJ off her back, but it would also irk him that the object of his scorn was the object of her affections.

But when Tom checked in with Octavia a couple of days later on the status of her problem, she told him that the situation had only gotten worse. Fired up with extreme jealousy and rivalry, the DJ was more determined than ever to make Octavia his conquest. Tom recommended a more extreme approach: He suggested Octavia tell the DJ that she and Tom were so much in love that they'd decided to get married the following week. That should do the trick. Of course, this was all a joke; Tom and Octavia weren't even friends.

The "news" about Tom and Octavia quickly spread throughout the club. The staff (except for the DJ, of course) were all wild about this romance that had happened right under their noses, and consequently they felt proprietary about the whole affair. One of the directors of the record company that owned the club (who is also someone that Tom now works with) heard about the impending marriage and bought the couple a surprise wedding gift of two gold rings. He also took it upon himself to apply for the marriage license and even booked the marriage registry to perform the ceremony in seven days' time. The management of the club pitched in, deciding to throw a reception for Tom and Octavia to be catered by the club's kitchen.

Tom and Octavia decided to go along with what they perceived as a dare. What the hell, they thought. They didn't take it seriously, it had started as a joke, it still was a joke, but the joke had taken on a life of its own. Who were they to stop it? They both thought the whole thing was hilarious, Tom in particular because he knew how angry the DJ would be. In the week before the wedding, Tom and Octavia became lovers. How difficult could it be to marry someone when sex was this good? Besides, Tom liked the idea of rescuing this damsel in distress, and she seemed to enjoy the rescue.

So marry they did. In keeping with what married people generally do, the two bought a house, a car, and a St. Bernard. This is what married people do, so why not? They were having great sex and having a great time playing house, so it certainly wasn't difficult to live together. They actually stayed together for two and a half years, a small miracle considering how their relationship began, but both eventually realized they didn't have a strong enough foundation to maintain a lifelong partnership.

Although the couple parted amiably, Octavia learned that while getting married on a dare can be fun, it would probably be best to put a bit more thought into choosing a husband the next time around. And despite Tom's less-than-serious approach to his first proposal, he maintains that he is a die-hard romantic and is currently searching for "the perfect princess" with whom he can join hands and hearts forever. His idea of the most passionate proposal a man can make? "If you say yes, I'll set fire to both of us. If you say no, I'll just set fire to myself." So watch out, ladies. This is a man definitely worth stoking the fires for.

everybody's business

meant to be

Tina, a marriage/family/child therapist and author of several self-help books, was giving a workshop with a very close male friend and colleague at a psychology convention. They had about twenty minutes to kill before their presentation was to begin, and noticed that across the hall a psychic was conducting a workshop. On a whim, they decided to drop in, and sat in the back of the room to satisfy their curiosity.

Within a minute, the psychic asked if there was anyone named Tina in the room. Tina raised her hand, a sort of anticipatory chill running down her spine. The psychic walked over to Tina and proceeded to tell her extremely accurate things about her family. If that weren't strange enough, the psychic then said, "I've been told to tell you something. I've been told that you're going to get rich in December and it's going to change your life."

A few months later, Tina met Richard, a ballroom dance instructor. Sparks flew immediately. This fateful meeting occurred just three days after Richard had bought a house, something he had dreamed of and saved for for years. Tina and Richard got seriously involved very quickly, and although Richard was happily in love, for him this meant not only sharing the house should they choose to make the big marriage commitment, but possibly losing it if it didn't work out. Both Tina and Richard were less than starry-eyed about the institution of marriage; both were divorced, and neither one of them ever wanted to get married again.

Tina's not a big believer in astrology, but with the same sort of open-minded curiosity that caused her to wander into the psychic workshop a few months earlier, she made an appointment for a reading with an astrologer friend. Although this was just ten days after she and Richard met, Tina asked Richard to accompany her. Tina laughs as she recalls that when the astrologer did comparison charts for the new couple, she "tripped all over herself trying not to say the 'M' word," because the inevitability of a blessedly happy marriage was just written all over their charts.

Surprisingly, neither Richard nor Tina was frightened by this reading. In fact, that night at dinner, Richard casually asked Tina if she thought they would eventually get married. "Probably," she said with feigned nonchalance, and added, "Are you going to ask me?" "Yeah, sometime," he replied.

Nothing more about future plans was mentioned until a couple of months later, when Richard decided to have a big housewarming party. Richard invited all of his friends, most of whom Tina hadn't met. "What would you say if I asked you to marry me at the party?" he asked. Tina said she'd probably say yes, but Richard would just have to ask her to find out. She knew she'd say yes, but she didn't want to give it away without being properly asked. Richard kept bugging her about it, but she remained cagey and mysterious.

At Richard's party, Tina noticed that for about the first two-thirds of the evening, Richard literally kept his distance from her. She didn't take it personally, though, because as a psychologist, she realized that he was behaving out of fear. Finally, Tina walked up to Richard as he was surveying the scene from his entranceway. "Remember me?" she asked coyly. Richard looked at her sheepishly and said that he just couldn't do it; he couldn't ask her. No problem, she reassured him. She hadn't asked him to, and it was all right.

That's all Richard needed to hear. He grabbed her and kissed her, and asked her to marry him, to which she immediately said yes. She was more than taken aback, however, when Richard instantly made a general announcement about his proposal to his party guests. There was dead silence, broken only by a wisecracking friend of Richard's who loudly quipped, "But it's OK, folks, she said no." Not even a laugh. You could have heard a pin drop, except for some of Richard's dance students who started crying. Not exactly the response Richard had hoped for.

Tina, who is quite a self-possessed and nonjudgmental

sort, realized what was going on. She was a complete stranger to most of these people, who only knew of her as the woman Richard had just begun seeing two months before. The only person who congratulated them that night was a former girlfriend of Richard's. The couple wasn't about to let the partygoers' funereal mood spoil their joy, and they decided to find the humor in the situation.

By the time they got married seven months later, Tina had won the hearts of all of Richard's friends, who pooled their communal efforts and resources to make their wedding a beautiful celebration of love as well as friendship.

Tina also finally realized the significance of the psychic's prediction. She did "get Rich in December." Richard, whose professional name was "Mr. Rich," proposed in December. And yes, it did indeed "change her life."

make an honest woman of her

They travel all over the world together and share a tremendous number of interests, including golf and bridge. The chemistry between them is tangible. They call each other "soulmates, two peas in a pod." They often make the same comment at the same moment. Irving and Estelle also find it unbelievable that they were lucky enough to meet.

How did they find each other? Irving's daughter, Lorilie, lived next door to Estelle's son, George, in Cherry Hill, New Jersey. When Lorilie's mother and George's father died within six months of each other, Lorilie and

George decided to introduce their respective surviving parents. But the timing, unfortunately, just wasn't right. Irving had just lost his beloved wife, and Estelle was grieving for her husband of many years. When they met for the first time at Estelle's grandson's birthday party, they didn't allow themselves to be attracted to each other. They were still adjusting to living in the world without their life partners. Irving, more recently widowed than Estelle, was even less ready to meet someone new.

Estelle lived in Florida, but Irving was still selling his house and putting his affairs in order. It would be some time before he would be settled in Florida, too. Lorilie told Estelle that when her father landed in the sunshine state, he would call her, but Estelle was doubtful. This handsome, eligible widower was sure to be snatched up before then.

For a while, it seemed as if Estelle and Irving were not meant to connect. Irving did call when he got to Florida, just before Thanksgiving, but Estelle was out of town. When she called him back, Irving was entertaining his visiting sister and was too busy to meet her. They remained phone buddies until January. It was then that Estelle developed a back problem and wasn't feeling great. The minute Irving heard that she was ailing, he decided it was time to meet her. However, she could not go out and was concerned about how she would entertain him. The doctor had ordered bedrest but allowed her to stay on the couch if Irving kept his visit brief.

Irving intended to stop by for an hour and stayed for four. By the time he left, they felt like old friends; it was as if they had always known each other. She learned from their conversation that they both loved the opera. The following week *Tosca* was to be televised, and they made plans to watch it together at Estelle's place.

When the opera ended and it was time to go, Irving left with a casual "Good-bye, I'll be in touch." As Estelle started to turn off the lights in preparation for bed, she saw his glasses in the den where they had been sitting. Despite her worry, she waited forty-five minutes to call, allowing him time to get home. She was very concerned because surely he'd be in as much trouble without his glasses as she would be without hers. Irving told her he didn't even realize he'd left his glasses and said he'd be back the next day to pick them up. But later he admitted that he'd left them on purpose to have an excuse to go back.

When Estelle was feeling better in March, she brought her eightysomething mother from Miami Beach to her home in Boca for a short visit. Mother fell head over heels for Irving, and Estelle claims that her mother became more interested in visiting with him than she was with Estelle.

As their relationship quickly progressed, Estelle and Irving traveled together for much of the next year and into the fall. When they returned to Florida, Irving moved into

Estelle's apartment. Keep in mind, now, that Irving was a retired senior citizen, and Estelle was just three years short of being one herself. They had adapted to the changing times and were quite content to cohabitate forevermore. Irving never planned to propose, which was just fine with Estelle. Estelle's living situation, however, did not sit well with her family.

It was a scandal. Intent on keeping her darling Irving in the family, Estelle's mother used all her not-so-subtle ammunition. At every opportunity, she asked him, "So when are you going to make an honest woman out of my daughter?"

To add to the pressure, Estelle's daughter-in-law joined the matrimonial crusade. She was somewhat conservative about such things and was quick to express her fears that the situation would set a poor example for her young son.

With all this hectoring, what could they do? The decision was made for them. Irving and Estelle were wed the next spring on Mother's Day. Between them they have twelve grandchildren, and they've been happily married for over ten years.

the fifth question

Newlyweds Brad and Debbie would never have met had it not been for Bruce, who directed a summer camp for United Synagogue Youth. It was Bruce who invited Brad to become a counselor for just eight days in the summer of 1990. Brad politely declined the offer, but Bruce sweetened the deal. He informed Brad that there was a lovely

counselor there named Debbie who seemed just right for
Brad, and Brad needed no further convincing. Off to summer camp he went.

Bruce, who should have played the Matchmaker in *Fid-
dler on the Roof*, couldn't have been more right. Debbie
cried on the eighth day of summer camp when it was time
for Brad to go home. She was just certain she would never
see him again. "I had been dumped many times before,"
she good-naturedly laments. Brad assured Debbie that this
was no short-term thing, but Debbie was very skeptical.
They were about to begin their junior years at colleges
that were a good five-hour drive apart, and during the
summer they would also be separated by quite a long distance. But neither distance nor phone rates nor the hefty
toll on the Throgs Neck Bridge could keep these two
lovebirds apart. They saw each other once or twice a
month during the school year, more during the summer,
and spoke on the phone constantly.

It became evident that they would get married, but
everyone wanted to know when—Debbie, especially. At
Debbie's brother's wedding, people kept asking. Debbie's
father, an accountant, insisted that he needed two tax seasons to recover from his son's wedding, and Brad, who
wasn't quite ready at the time, was happy to wait. Despite
Debbie's nudging, he maintained that this decision was
not hers, that how and when he proposed was his decision
entirely and she was not to be involved in it. Debbie dis-
agreed; she wanted to know everything. But Brad, whose
stubbornness was stronger than Debbie's persistence,
would not be swayed. He was determined to create the
perfect proposal, and such things take time. Meanwhile, at
every Yankee game the two attended, Debbie would

spend the entire game staring at the scoreboard looking for her proposal. Brad would have been amused by this had he known, but he was an adamant sports fan and was too busy watching the games to see what Debbie was up to.

In January, Brad eventually came up with his three-month plan. His first obstacle was getting a ring without Debbie finding out. This was no small task because they kept close tabs on each other's whereabouts and spoke on the phone every day. Meanwhile, Brad was becoming an expert on diamonds and went to several shops before selecting just the one he wanted. He also managed to get Debbie's ring size by tracing one of her rings while she was in the shower.

The day in February when Brad took off from work to pick up the ring started the most difficult month of his life. Brad had shared everything with Debbie for so many years but was now about to keep from her the most important thing of his whole life. While he was getting the ring, Debbie called Brad at work and was surprised to find he wasn't there. Brad's coworker, thinking fast, said Brad was at the dentist. Debbie was very worried because she knew for a fact that Brad was not going to the dentist that day—it must be an emergency! Debbie's coworker tried to soothe Debbie. She jokingly told her not to bother Brad because perhaps he was out buying her a diamond ring. When Debbie asked Brad that night where he had been, he told her he had been shopping with his mother, which to Debbie seemed even stranger than going to the dentist. But she was relieved that Brad was all right and didn't think to question his veracity.

By March, the very elaborate plan was in place. Debbie's mother was hosting the second Passover seder and, as Brad expected, for the second year in a row invited Brad's entire family, including Brad's parents, uncle, grandmother, and siblings—who until that day were the only ones in on the plan. Brad was with Debbie all day but did not have the ring with him for fear that Debbie would find it. Instead he had his mother bring it, and according to Brad's specific instructions, she marched right into the bathroom and left it on the counter while Brad guarded the bathroom door, looking to all the world as if he was very eager to be next (which he was). Good thing no one suggested he use the upstairs bathroom! In the bathroom, Brad planted the ring in his sock so that Debbie would not accidentally rub up against it as she nuzzled against him at the seder table.

With the ring now in hand (or to be more precise, on ankle), it was now an hour before dinner. Brad's mother, the happy accomplice, distracted Debbie by asking to be shown old photographs in Debbie's upstairs bedroom so that Brad could slip into the basement with Debbie's parents. There, with their undivided attention, he earnestly asked, "If it's OK with you, tonight I would like to ask Debbie to be my wife." As they embraced with great joy, he made them promise not to tell other members of Debbie's family, and they gladly complied.

Debbie recalls how she stumbled upon the two mothers-in-law-to-be talking in hushed voices through tears. She wasn't fazed by the sight, for the women had become close and often shared emotional stories. Debbie asked what was up, and they both said "nothing."

During Passover, there is always a good deal of anticipation for the festive meal, usually because everyone is hungry. But this particular holy night, there was much more going on around the seder table. Brad, who had already waited three months, could hardly wait three minutes more—not for the festive meal but for "the four questions," which is a ritual reading traditionally performed by the youngest at the table. In this case, the task fell to Debbie's cousin Ronnie, who was twelve at the time, and who didn't have a clue that she was about to make history. When Ronnie finished asking the four questions, which call for an explanation of the Passover holiday, Brad said to her, "You're forgetting the fifth question." Now Ronnie may have been only twelve, but she had been around the Passover block a few times, and she was completely baffled—as was Debbie who kept turning to her cousin and saying, "What in the world is he doing?" Ronnie just sat there looking completely puzzled, because she'd never heard of any fifth question in Hebrew school. At this point, Brad launched into what amounted to a sermon: "Passover and the four questions have a theme: Why is tonight different from all nights? You might think that tonight is different because we have matzo, and tonight might be different because we eat bitter herbs, and tonight might be different because we have all these people here [these are the standard answers], but the real reason tonight is different from all other nights is because tonight there's a fifth question."

Continuing, Brad then got down on one knee beside the seder table and said, "The fifth question is, I want to know if Debbie will be my wife."

Still completely clueless, Debbie turned to her cousin and again asked what Brad was doing.

Brad said, "I'm proposing to you" and asked Debbie to

close her eyes as he discreetly removed the ring from his sock.

The truth of what was happening didn't dawn on Debbie until she saw the ring. As she sat there speechless, Debbie's brother Paul yelled out, "I didn't hear an answer!" to which Debbie finally was able to reply through her emotions, "Yes!" Everyone hugged and applauded, and Debbie was especially happy that the most important people in her life were there in the room, those whom she would have immediately called had she been alone with Brad. Despite her protests and insistence to know everything, this proposal could not have been more perfect for her, and she would not have wanted it any other way.

And so it was, two tax seasons later, that Debbie's dad heartily joined the congregation's booming chorus as Brad smashed the glass beneath his foot: *Mazel Tav*! (Congratulations!)

a bit of romance and a bit of luck

Barbara, a nice Jewish girl from New York, had never had much confidence in her success with men. Her dream was to meet a good man and get married. Or was that the dream of her domineering mother, the woman who had paid the dry cleaner's son to take Barbara to her high school prom? In two years of college, Barbara never even had a date, despite the fact that women made up far less than 1 percent of the student population at her formerly all-male, Catholic college.

In that very parochial atmosphere, Barbara found refuge

in Sue, another native New Yorker who became her best friend. They left school and took an apartment together in Manhattan, but when Sue met a man and got engaged, the pressure to meet a mate was on again for Barbara. Sue had a brilliant idea: She would fix Barbara up with the president of the company where she worked. However, when Sue approached the president with her plan, he was obliged to decline, for he was to be married in a month. He did, however, happen to have an identical twin brother who happened to be single. The blind date was a success, and Barbara and Evan quickly became an item.

Barbara hoped for a proposal on every holiday and occasion, but none came. One day, Barbara was to meet Evan in front of his apartment in Manhattan. When she got there, a cab was waiting for them and already knew their destination. Barbara didn't, and was certainly surprised when they were dropped off at the Plaza Hotel, where Evan had a reservation. When they arrived in their room, Evan got down on one knee and proposed. Needless to say, Barbara happily accepted, despite the fact that in place of a ring she got a Tiffany's box with an IOU inside. (If only she'd landed the rich twin!)

Since jobs in Evan's medical administration field were scarce in New York, and Barbara was more than happy to put three thousand miles between herself and her mother, the newly engaged couple moved to Los Angeles. Evan found the jobs in Los Angeles to be even scarcer, but Barbara found that parental distance was better than New York cheesecake. Eager to find the financial means to get married, Evan applied to be a contestant on several game shows and managed to get on *Wheel of Fortune*. He won big prizes, including a honeymoon (a trip to Acapulco), a ring (a Tiffany's gift certificate), and a wedding cake (a five-hundred-dollar bakery gift certificate). He told Barbara that they might as well get married right away, and they did. When they got back from their honeymoon, however, the nuptial apartment had been burgled by a decidedly unromantic thief, who had absconded with the remainder of Evan's game-show spoils.

Eighteen years later, the two are happily married and happily employed, although Barbara often gripes about Evan's lack of romantic inclinations. His customary, bewildered reply is to remind her about his legendary proposal in the Plaza Hotel. To this, she responds that there is a statute of limitations on such things and hopes he'll get the hint.

a way with words

lucky thirteen

It would be an understatement to say that Mike Baron plays Scrabble. The serious Scrabble-playing world has initiated a Hall of Fame, and Mike, who founded a Scrabble club in Albuquerque, was one of the first inductees. To promote the game, Mike has been on *Good Morning America* with Erma Bombeck, interviewed on television by *E!* magazine, heard on National Public Radio's *All Things Considered*, and has made numerous other appearances locally, nationally, and even internationally. It's only fitting that he would meet his one true love at a Scrabble tournament.

Although Pamina Deutsch had been playing Scrabble for many years, she did not meet Mike until 1988 at one of her first tournaments, the Reno Western Scrabble Championships. Mike had his eye on that lovely woman from Seattle during the whole tournament and was lucky enough to obtain her address when the tournament ended (she had filled out a form to buy a word-list book from him).

Coincidentally, Mike was scheduled to visit his brother in the neighboring city of Portland right after the tournament. He took the opportunity to visit Pamina in Seattle, where they both played in another Scrabble tournament a few weeks after that. Flushed with the happiness and inspiration of a young man in love, Mike won that tournament, and Pamina did very well in her division as well.

From Albuquerque to Los Angeles to Durango to the Grand Canyon, over the next thirteen months they met thirteen times at Scrabble tournaments all over the United States. On their thirteenth meeting, thirteen months later in September 1989, Mike was to play the state Scrabble champion in an exhibition game at the annual Bumbershoot Festival in Seattle.

Thinking the game would be televised, Mike devised a unique plan. From Albuquerque to Seattle, he carried in his pocket the Scrabble tiles that would spell out "Will you marry me?" It was his intention that during the end of the game, while the cameras were rolling, in front of Pamina's entire community, he would pull out the tiles and lay them on the board. When the end game arrived, he did not see any floodlights, and, assuming the game was not being televised, he left the tiles in his pocket. Well, it turned out the game *was* indeed televised, and Mike was very disappointed that he had missed his chance.

Mike went to Pamina's house the next day. He was to leave that day and did not want to go home with the tiles that had traveled sixteen hundred miles for a very specific purpose. While Pamina was in the next room, Mike laid out the tiles on a Scrabble board that was on the table. When Pamina saw them, she was very surprised and delighted but felt she needed time to think about it. This time Mike's disappointment was tinged with relief that he hadn't proposed on television!

A couple of days later, while Mike was out playing Scrabble at the Albuquerque club, his answering machine was recording the best message he was ever to receive. In the words of Molly Bloom (James Joyce's *Ulysses*), Pamina's voice proclaimed, "Yes, yes, a thousand times yes."

Cut to the present: Leave it to Mike to figure out that their baby daughter's name (Melina Gabriella Baron-Deutsch) anagrams to "I am a hot, lean, nude, Scrabble girl."

lucky seven

Meanwhile, across the continent in Newton, Massachusetts, at about the same time that Pamina and Mike were hunched over their Scrabble boards at the Grand Canyon, Susan and Lewis were off to play Scrabble at a friend's house. Unlike Pamina and Mike, Susan and Lewis were not serious about Scrabble—except to say that it's the thing that brought them together. They played for a few months and then stopped. Sometime after that, they started dating.

On their seven-month anniversary of dating, which co-incided with Lewis's grandparents' sixty-seventh wedding anniversary (and which Lewis decided *must* be a lucky day), Lewis set up his deluxe Scrabble board in the box in his apartment. He used tape to make sure the tiles would stay in place if the board were accidentally knocked over.

Susan came over after dinner, and he invited her to play Scrabble for old time's sake. Susan wasn't sure she wanted to play, but Lewis persuaded her. She opened the box, while Lewis looked on anxiously.

Susan was surprised to see "$S_1U_1S_1A_1N_1$, $W_4I_1L_1L_1$ $Y_4O_1U_1$ $M_3A_1R_1R_1Y_4$ M_3E_1," along with the tiles needed to spell out either answer. She knew what she wanted to say, but there was no "y" to use for saying yes—Lewis had used up all of the available "y"'s in the proposal ("*you*" and "marr*y*"). He had, however, left her a blank tile with which to answer in the affirmative. She didn't want to give an ambiguous response, so she replaced the "y" in "you" with her blank and took the "y" for her "yes" response.

Now it's over seven years later, and Lewis still enjoys complaining to Susan that she will not let anyone play on their lovely deluxe set. She fully intends to frame it some-day. It still reads, "Susan, will -ou marry me." The "no" tiles are forever confined to the bag.

And if they, or anyone else, want to know what their little boy's name anagrams into, they'll have to call Mike and Pamina. Our guess is that you would find it in the letters "$H_4A_1P_3P_3I_1L_1Y_4$ $E_1V_4E_1R_1$ $A_1F_3T_1E_1R_1$."

love, the ultimate
contact sport

their one hundredth game together

After they'd been dating for a couple of years, David and Shirra talked about eventually getting married. Both avid baseball fans, they'd made attending baseball games a mainstay of their courtship, and David said that he'd propose to Shirra at their one hundredth game. They'd been to so many games that Shirra had lost track, but David had already figured out exactly how many they'd attended. He told Shirra they were up to about eighty games already, but only he knew the exact number was seventy-eight. He wanted some element of surprise, and Shirra didn't mind indulging him.

When it was time for their one hundredth game, David led Shirra to believe that they'd only reached the high nineties. Meanwhile, he'd spent several weeks doing some elaborate planning to infuse as much as possible of the unexpected into the expected one hundredth game proposal.

David arranged for twenty-six of their respective family and friends to attend the one hundredth game, all without Shirra's knowledge. The night of the one hundredth game, their favorite team, the Yankees, were playing the Red Sox at Yankee Stadium. He deliberately seated himself and Shirra in the wrong section of the stadium, while their expectant party waited in another section.

Before the game, Shirra had been working on a crossword puzzle, and if there's one thing that drove her crazy, it was when David would fill in answers for her. When they got to the stadium, Shirra excused herself to powder her nose, warning David to keep his hands off her crossword puzzle. When she returned to her seat, she was annoyed to find that David had filled in some boxes. On closer examination, she saw that he'd written "100TH GAME. I LOVE YOU." It was then that she realized that this was in fact their one hundredth game. David asked Shirra right then to marry him, and she happily accepted with many hugs and kisses. But where was the ring? she wondered. David explained that he didn't have the ring with him, and Shirra accepted this good-naturedly. She started eating the customary box of Cracker Jacks that David had given her, and noticed that the prize seemed to be a bit more substantial in weight than the usual one. Indeed it was, for inside the package was a gorgeous diamond engagement ring. Shirra was again thrilled and surprised.

For about the last twenty games or so, David had established a pattern of suggesting he and Shirra move to better seats, and had even at times deliberately taken the wrong seats, so that an usher might end up moving them to the right section to correct his "error." So this night, when David suggested he and Shirra move to another section, she thought nothing was strange about it. She was stunned when they arrived at their new seats and saw her and David's family and friends waiting for them and applauding. Shirra happily showed off her new ring. But the surprises weren't over yet.

David had often complained to Shirra that he thought the stadium's electronic "Fan Marquee" was boring and a waste of money, so he knew she'd never expect what came next. After the Fan Marquee flashed and the announcer announced five of the usual "Happy Anniversary, so-and-so's," and with hardly a reaction from the jaded fans in the packed stadium, the final marquee message proclaimed: "SHIRRA, ON THIS OUR 100TH GAME TOGETHER PLEASE SAY YOU'LL MARRY ME. DAVID." Thousands of fans exploded in cheers and shouts, and Shirra and David's joy was complete. David basked in his triumph at making his proposal to Shirra not only romantic but suspenseful and fun. Besides, their favorite Yankee hit the game-winning home run that night.

HOT TIP FOR AMOROUS YANKEE FANS: If you'd like to pop the question via the Yankee Stadium Fan Marquee, it costs only about twenty-five dollars, which is donated to the Leukemia Society. Your request must be made in writing to Yankee Stadium several weeks in advance, and the limit is about twelve words.

oh, say can you see that i love you?

Talk about coincidences. Andrew and Karen both attended George Washington National Law Center, although Andrew graduated before Karen even started. They both loved to perform as singers in the annual variety show—albeit in different years. And they both lived in the same building at the same time in Arlington, Virginia.

Two years after Andrew graduated, he attended the annual variety show. He was particularly impressed with one woman whose remarkable voice captivated him. After the show he waited for her, and when she walked past him, the cleverest thing he could think of to say was, "You were really good tonight." "Thank you," Karen responded without even breaking stride.

They didn't speak again for another year, and they still didn't realize they lived in the same building. In February of 1994, two days before the next variety show, Andrew ran into Karen in his building and made a little small talk. She was carrying a big sewing machine, and he thought she was cute. Although he didn't realize this was the singer he had admired, he did vaguely recognize her from the building. He asked what the sewing machine was for, and she said it was for the school show. Andrew assumed she was the show seamstress and bragged about his role in prior shows. They said good-bye politely.

Two days later, he attended the show. There on the stage was the woman of his dreams singing a very funny legal parody to the tune of "A Whole New World." Andrew was completely mesmerized by Karen, but he still did not recognize that she was the same woman from his building.

After the show he went to the cast party determined to meet her. He waited around until she started talking to someone he knew, and then he made his move. He walked up and started talking to the man he knew so that he could insinuate himself into the conversation with her. He employed the same clever conversation opener he had used the year before: "You were really great tonight." When the mutual friend began to introduce them with "Andy, this is Karen," Karen declared, "Oh, I know you. You live in my building!" Andrew felt like a complete moron, because until that moment he had thought the woman in his building was the seamstress. They talked a few moments and then said goodnight.

The next day, Andrew went out and bought the *Aladdin* CD so he could listen to "A Whole New World" over and over again. He couldn't get the song or Karen out of his mind. He wanted to ask her out but was too nervous. He never got up the nerve to act, but Karen saved him. Two months later, they ran into each other in their building parking lot. Karen had just returned from New York and was pulling into the garage. She rolled down her window and, without any forethought, asked, "What are you doing? Do you want to catch a movie?"

They had a rocky start and didn't quite click until September. But then things started turning around for them, and their relationship began to get serious. One of the things they enjoyed doing was singing together. Karen is a midsoprano, and Andy is a tenor. For these two lawyers, singing is a serious hobby, although Andrew modestly proclaims, "She's real good; I'm not; I sing in the shower; she sings with bands."

Consistent with her forthrightness in asking him out, Karen was the first to say "I love you," but she was determined not to be the one to propose or buy the ring. On New Year's Eve they both realized this might be it. It became a foregone conclusion that they were going to get married, but that year was a hectic one. Karen graduated from law school and went to Europe with her college roommate for three weeks. While Karen was away, Andrew went to New Jersey and picked out the ring. She had given him explicit instructions on what she wanted: a round stone, six baguettes, a platinum band. But there was still the question of when he would give it to her. He decided it would be at the end of the year in December, during the week between their two birthdays.

The Friday before Thanksgiving, Karen got a call from the U.S. Air Arena where the Washington Capitals play hockey. Would Karen sing the national anthem on Tuesday night? Yes, of course, she'd be thrilled to do it.

Andrew was having trouble thinking of a way to surprise Karen with a proposal, because he knew she was expecting the ring—no matter when he gave it to her. Andrew had a flash of inspiration. He asked his friend who worked for the Capitals if he could come out on the blue carpet that they roll out in the middle of the ice and get down on one knee and propose there (which was the complete opposite of what he had been planning—a traditional romantic, private dinner). But this opportunity couldn't be missed. Still, he needed to be reassured that it would be romantic. He conducted a straw poll of everyone he knew. Was this romantic? Almost everyone said it would be terrific. A few women said it was a horrible idea—a hockey game?!! Still other people offered additional suggestions, "Why don't you get on the Zamboni [the machine they clean the ice with] and ride in like a knight?"

In the meantime, the Capitals called back and said that for reasons of liability he couldn't walk out on the ice. Nevertheless, they were very nice about it, saying they would be willing to work with him to make the proposal special. What they planned was that when she finished singing, as she came off the ice, she would go through the penalty box to the corner of the arena to a big open area where he would be waiting, and they would keep the camera on her.

On Sunday, Andrew drove to Delaware and met his parents halfway between their homes at a rest stop. He says it felt like some sort of clandestine drug deal: Andrew gave them the money, and they gave him the ring. He went for a short time to a Washington Redskins game to establish his alibi. Karen had no idea the exchange took place.

On Monday, the day before the Capitals game, Andrew persuaded his sister Ellen and his friend Verne to drive to the game with them so that Karen would be thrown farther off the track. They all went to the arena in the same car. When they arrived, Karen went off to practice with the organist. It was as if everyone in the arena except Karen knew that he was proposing that evening. The security guards would come up to him and say, "So you're the guy, huh?" When he said, "How did you know?" They replied, "We know everything."

The arena was starting to fill up. Andrew got nervous

and asked if he could use one of the bathrooms. He was escorted into the bathroom in the team locker room where he met two more guards. One looked at Andrew and said, "Hey, you can still change your mind." When Andrew asked, "How did you know?" The guard responded, "Hey, we all know."

As Andrew emerged from the bathroom, Karen was being escorted out onto the ice. Her face was on the four big video screens for all seventeen thousand people to behold. Meanwhile, Andrew was too nervous to even listen to Karen sing. Ellen and Verne had worked their way down the aisle with their camera. Karen was singing "and the home of the brave," and Andrew couldn't even hear the words over the thunderous pounding of his heart.

Karen walked off the ice straight into Andrew's arms. He gave her a hug and asked if she had been nervous. "No," she said. "Not really." He confessed about his own nervousness. Then he told her how he had loved her since the first time he heard her sing and that he couldn't wait to hear her sing at their wedding. Andrew got down on his knee, opened the ring box, and somewhere in the midst of all this Karen realized what was going on. She started trembling. As everyone in the stadium watched and the cameras remained fixed on them, Andrew took out the ring and put it on her finger. One cynical spectator with a beer yelled out, "Don't do it, Dude," which they have preserved for posterity on the videotape.

Andrew asked, "Will you be my wife?" and Karen hugged him for two or three minutes saying, "Oh my God, Oh my God, Oh my God." Andrew backed up and asked, "Is this a yes?" and Karen managed to say "Yes" although she was crying hysterically and extremely surprised. Everyone was clapping and yelling. Verne and Ellen were right there watching, and they were crying and screaming and clapping, too.

Neither Andrew nor Karen wanted to stay for the game. Andrew told Karen that Ellen and Verne had another way home and then brought her outside, walked past his own car directly into a big, black stretch limo. One of Andrew's friends, Maryanne, had told him that the proposal was not enough. It was the whole evening that would count. In the limo was a bottle of Dom Perignon. Andrew was still so nervous that he couldn't even pop the cork; the limo driver had to pull over and open it for them. They had dinner at The Prime Rib in Washington D.C. (in Andrew's opinion, the most elegant restaurant in town). The rest of the evening was spent eating, crying, and calling relatives. Thank goodness Andrew had called Karen's mother, Paula, the day before to ask permission, because when Karen called her she was crying so hard that a waiter tried to hand her a box of tissues.

After dinner, Andrew asked the limo driver to stop at the Iwo Jima memorial where the pair had gone on their way home from the movies on their very first date. This was where they had their first kiss. Now it was about midnight. Andrew took the ring off Karen's finger and told her that this was where he had intended to propose. Now that he wasn't so nervous, he wanted to do it one more time. And so he proposed again. Then he put the ring back on Karen's finger and told her not to take it off ever again. They kissed again, and the limo driver took them home to their two apartments in the same building.

tales of the shy and reluctant

tune-up, oil change, marriage

Susan, a college freshman, was very much in love with her first serious boyfriend, an engineering student named Bill, even if he did tend to ramble on endlessly about his passion for troubleshooting car problems.

One sunny autumn day on a break between classes, the two sat together under a canopy of enormous elm trees that were carpeting the campus with gorgeous red and gold leaves. While Bill elaborated on the details of repairing the crank case in his car that coming weekend, Susan amused herself by watching the leaves lazily drift down. She dreamily nodded and murmured in response as Bill talked on and on. Having no idea what a crank case was, in her mind Susan created some black, vaguely rectangular shape covered in dirty old motor oil. Bill continued going into interminable detail, completely unaware that Susan had no understanding of or interest in auto mechanics.

As Susan's eyes took in the breathtaking autumn hues, she didn't notice when, in the midst of Bill's diatribe on crank cases, he asked, without the slightest segue, "So, do you want to get married?" Susan continued to nod and act as if she were paying attention, until Bill gently shook her arm and repeated his proposal. Shaken out of her reverie, Susan looked at Bill's face, which looked extremely nervous and vulnerable at that moment, and she realized he was serious. Overcome with love as well as surprise, she instantly said yes. They kissed and held each other, and five months later they were married.

you *will* marry me

Erika and her boyfriend Klaus had been broken up for six months, and it was not the first time the pair had parted in the eight turbulent years they'd been together. In the class-conscious small-town Austrian society in which Erika and Klaus lived, marriage had always been out of the question for them. Although she was a successful attorney, Erika's middle-class background had always been unacceptable to Klaus's wealthy, aristocratic family. In all the years they'd been an on-again, off-again couple, Erika had never once been invited to Klaus's parents' home, and when Klaus's father, himself a lawyer, would run into Erika at court, he would greet her with no more cordiality than he would any casual colleague. Although the idea of not marrying suited Erika's desire for freedom from the traditional constraints of small-town Austrian married women, the snubs she received from Klaus's family had been a constant point of contention between them.

Needless to say, Erika was taken aback when one Saturday Klaus unexpectedly phoned her to invite her to breakfast the next morning at his parents' home. Although the two were on speaking terms since the breakup, Erika had become involved with another man. Klaus, too, had a new girlfriend, and Erika had heard a rumor that Klaus had applied for a marriage license to marry his girlfriend. So, when Klaus stood up at his family's breakfast table the next morning to make a "marriage announcement," Erika fully expected to get formal confirmation of what she had heard. Klaus then announced that he was to marry in two weeks' time, and that the ceremony would take place in a little Austrian village. As Erika listened to this news, she wondered why Klaus's wedding would be in the village where she was born. She knew that his new girlfriend hadn't been born in her hometown.

Erika then asked who the bride was, and Klaus replied that he wasn't finished with his announcement yet. He then said that a week after the wedding, he and his new wife would be moving to the United States. Klaus then handed Erika a passport. She looked at it and saw that it bore her first name and his last name. Startled and confused, she asked him if this was a joke. No, he said, we are going to be married in two weeks, my parents have agreed, and we will be moving to the United States. To punctuate his point, he handed Erika a private investigator's report on her own activities and background, to show that Klaus had checked her out to his parents' satisfaction.

After all the pain she'd endured in their relationship, Erika was afraid to open her heart again to Klaus. Despite her emphatic objections to this proposal, which more closely resembled a hostile corporate takeover than a declaration of love, Klaus and his family insisted she had no choice, saying that it was all official and already quite public. Indeed, they had placed announcements in the newspapers that day. Feeling overwhelmed by pressure and shock, Erika said she had to at least discuss the matter with her parents. No problem, Klaus replied, they're on their way over here. A half hour later, Erika's parents showed up, and the two sets of parents planned the wedding together while she sat there in stunned disbelief.

Erika never actually said yes, not at the breakfast table that fateful morning, and not at the church. But marry him she did. So why did she go through with it? Quite simply, her clever suitor made her an offer he knew she couldn't refuse. Erika had always dreamed of escaping the chokehold of her provincial Austrian life and making a new start in the United States, and marrying Klaus ultimately seemed like a fair price to pay. And although on the surface this certainly wasn't the most romantic proposal she could have imagined, she realized that Klaus's only motivation to move to this country was to win her heart. In time, he did.

it's no skin off my nose

Christie and John were friends for three years, acting together in a theater company, before they became romantically entangled. Christie was involved in a rather unhealthy relationship with another man, and never noticed the way John would look at her at rehearsals. Despite Christie's unavailability, John always knew in his heart that he and Christie would someday be together. He didn't think Christie's boyfriend was good enough for her, but he prudently kept those feelings to himself, remaining a supportive friend and colleague.

About three days after Christie's boyfriend unceremoniously dumped her in a restaurant, John told her of his strong feelings for her. Christie was determined to nurse her hurt feelings and remain single for at least ten years, but John quickly convinced her that she'd just wasted two years on a jerk, so why waste another ten? She could hardly dispute John's logic. After three blissful months with John, they were spending the evening in Christie's apartment, and John asked if he could run downstairs and "bring up a few things." He quickly reappeared with all of his clothes and a television. Christie was shocked speechless. They'd never even broached the subject of living together, and Christie wasn't quite sure how to react to all this. However, in her typical, lifelong pattern of letting things happen to her without making conscious choices, she decided to go along with it anyway. Christie wasn't in love with John at this point, but she liked him very much. He was kind and good to her, and had certainly helped her get through the pain of her recent breakup.

Marriage was definitely out of the question for both Christie and John. He looked at the institution as the government's way of collecting taxes; she looked at it as a way for men to enslave women. They progressed nicely in their living situation, and after a couple of more months,

Christie began to realize that she was in love. She also began to get involved in the study of the Bible, an interest that John, an atheist, did not share. Their religious differences caused no problems at all in their relationship, until Christie learned that "fornication" was something that people who lived by the principles of the Bible were not supposed to do.

Christie had always thought that "fornication" meant having sex with someone whose name and address remained a mystery, but when she looked up the dictionary definition, she realized it meant sex between two people who were not married to each other. She thought about it at some length and decided that after living with three different men, two of which relationships had ended badly, she might as well try something new. With no thought of marrying John, she announced to him that her involvement in her new religion precluded any continued "fornication." John was floored by this unexpected turn of events. He accused her of being brainwashed, even of insanity, but there was no swaying her. And John was not going to be pressured into marrying her, which Christie honestly protested she had no intention of doing. She loved John, but they both figured he'd have to move out. They couldn't revert to being platonic friends, and she wouldn't continue sleeping with him.

Although determined to stay true to her adopted faith, Christie was torn. She knew she was risking the loss of the one man whose integrity and imagination had captivated her affections, and this for an abstract concept, but she had to give it a try. John found his own apartment and began packing to move out. When he was all packed, John sat down on a pile of boxes, looking quite disturbed. Christie asked him what was the matter, and he said, "I want to be with you. You're the one I want, and I don't need a piece of paper to make it right." Christie countered that it was not about a piece of paper, it was about living life by the principles espoused in this book she believed in. She told him he was free to live his own life in any way he chose, but she owed it to herself to live her life the way she chose.

John sat there silently for a while, then said, "So if I want to be with you, what would I have to do?" Christie then tentatively replied, "I guess you'd have to marry me . . . ? Or we could be friends . . . ?" She didn't really think she could be friends, but she couldn't imagine never seeing John again. She was terrified, felt as if she were standing on the edge of a cliff about to jump off, not knowing whether she would fall or fly. All she could do was have faith that whatever happened would be for her highest good.

John went into the closet to get the rest of his things, and presently, Christie heard the muffled sound of his voice emanating from the depths of the closet. "OK, I'll marry you," he said. "It's no skin off my nose."

Although this was certainly not the most eloquent proposal, Christie only needed to look at John's face to realize that this was a declaration of love, not of resignation. She had already accepted that she would have to give him up, and never expected that he would marry her. They held each other close, and she silently promised herself that she would do everything in her power to ensure that neither one of them ever regretted taking this step. Many years later, they continue to have one of the happiest, romantic marriages anyone could hope for.

lady's choice

Jerry and Sharon met as students at the University of Miami in the fall of 1986. Friends from the start, they never dated—even to this day. All the time they were in college, Sharon had a thing for Jerry, but he was completely unaware of it. They would go out together, but it was just as friends, although neither of them dated anyone else. Sharon never met anyone she liked more than Jerry, and he never met anyone he wanted to go out with. More accurately, he could never imagine that anyone would want to go out with him.

In 1988, Sharon graduated and moved to Texas and Jerry stayed in Florida. Although they parted ways, they stayed in touch on the Internet. They would spend an hour or two on-line nearly every day. They would tell each other how the day went; she would ask him how to fix her car; they would both complain about difficult people at work. And Jerry would report to Sharon about his mother's unflagging efforts to fix him up with women.

It was Jerry's mother's personal crusade to find a woman for her son. She'd set him up on blind dates, and he'd always behave terribly to make sure his dates didn't like him. This was the routine: Jerry would spend two hours convincing his dates that they hated him. It wouldn't have been so bad, but Jerry's mom tended to describe her son as a cross between Tom Selleck and Albert Schweitzer. The sheer look of disappointment on their faces when they answered the door was enough to put a huge damper on the evening. And this would add to Jerry's already low self-esteem.

Jerry reported these stories to his e-mail buddy Sharon, not realizing how jealous they would make her feel. He and Sharon were just friends, after all, he thought. Jerry was not ugly, stupid, and unlovable, she thought. After all, she loved him.

In the four years of their e-mail friendship, Sharon had only seen Jerry briefly when she visited her folks in Florida at Christmastime. This could not go on, she thought. Now he was turning thirty, and he still hadn't met anybody. She had to act.

For Jerry's thirtieth birthday in 1992, Sharon sent him a bouquet of black roses, a bunch of black balloons, and a card that read, "Neither one of us is getting any younger; let's get hitched." To Jerry this came completely out of the blue; it must be a joke. But Sharon had never been more serious in her life, and she was worried sick over how Jerry would respond. What she had done had taken a tremendous amount of courage. Still, she swore to herself that if Jerry said no, she was going to make him say yes eventually. But Jerry said neither yes nor no; he simply didn't answer.

They continued to correspond on-line for many months, and still Jerry did not respond to the proposal. Sometime during that period of time, Jerry began to realize that Sharon's proposal had been genuine, but he kept inventing reasons that they shouldn't be married, and Sharon kept trying to talk him into it. He simply could not accept that anyone would want him.

But he couldn't stop the inevitable. Sharon was in Los Angeles during the January 1994 earthquake. More than anything, Jerry realized how afraid he was of losing her. He realized at once that he loved her despite the fact that he had not seen her for some time.

Less than a month later, about a year after her proposal, Sharon had her wisdom teeth extracted. She bemoaned in her e-mails that she was having uncontrollable hiccups caused by the painkiller. Jerry responded with a one-word e-mail: "YES." Sharon wrote back "very funny," to which Jerry responded with another "YES." That's all he said, "yes." He jokes that he just wanted to scare her out of the hiccups.

It would be two more months until they would physically embrace. Shortly after the engagement, Jerry picked out a ring for Sharon. When he started e-mailing little smiley faces, she knew he had it and begged him to FedEx it to her so she could wear it right away. Usually a passive sort, Jerry would not give in this time. He wanted to give it to her in person. And he did, two months after the engagement, fourteen months after the proposal, and sixteen months since they had seen each other in person.

the test

It was the summer of 1979, and it was Valerie's last day as the lunch truck driver on a construction site in California. Men were always asking for her phone number, but instead of giving it to them she would take theirs and throw it in a shoe box. At the end of every week, she would dump out the contents of the box.

It was David's first day on the site. When he asked for

Valerie's number, she blurted out the name of a relative with whom she was staying. Thinking the number to be unlisted, she told him to look it up. To put it bluntly, in her own words, she "blew him off."

Valerie's policy was never to date a guy that she met on the job—David was to be the only exception to this rule. She was recovering from an abusive marriage and a nasty divorce. Also, she had a little daughter and just couldn't deal with dating.

Despite the fact that the name Valerie had given him was hard to pronounce and spell, David miraculously got the number; moreover, he found it in the Pomona phone book, even though the two had met in another town, Endora. He called the next day. Valerie didn't want to commit to a date, but her sister told her to be decisive: Either tell David not to call again or else go out with him.

Valerie reluctantly agreed to go to her first baseball game with David. She tried without success to find a chaperone, and on the night of the date she waited for David on her neighbor's front lawn, nervously drinking beer. Finally, David drove up in his truck. He was a large, muscular man with long bushy hair and a goatee. Valerie was twenty-three years old and only ninety-eight pounds—she thought she would just die if she got in his truck.

By the time David arrived, Valerie wasn't completely sober, but she wasn't slurring her words either. Mostly she was just extremely nervous. David was all smiles. At the game, they sat in a precarious place where the ball frequently flew at them. Valerie kept trying to run away, but the crowd scrunched her in. Meanwhile, David had a good time and thought Valerie was a lot of fun.

On the way home, Valerie's worst nightmare came

true. David got lost, and somehow they ended up at the beach. It was dark, and Valerie was certain that this seemingly nice man was going to turn out to be a serial killer.

He swore that he had not gotten lost intentionally. To this day, she still doesn't quite believe him. Nonetheless, everything seemed innocent enough. He didn't even try to kiss her. As they found their way home, she began to relax. They talked a lot, and he told her he had two daughters whom he was raising alone. Valerie could relate, because she and her sisters were raised exclusively by their father. This disclosure completely changed her outlook on David. He wasn't Jeffrey Dahmer after all; he was just like her dad.

They then went to pick up his daughters at the babysitter's house. She thought they were like two little baby dolls—two sweet girls ages six and nine. Valerie simply fell in love with them. She and David put the kids to bed and went to bed themselves.

They fell right into "couple mode," but before she would consider getting truly serious, he would have to pass a battery of stringent tests to prove that he was truly as good a man as he seemed. This time Valerie was not going to get married just for love. Having been burned so badly in her last relationship, she no longer believed what men said. It was how they behaved that counted.

The first test was this: Valerie bought a drum kit at a garage sale, and she set it up in David's house. Every day when David got home from work, she would go there and play her drums very loudly for two or three hours. She said she wanted to learn to be a drummer, that it was important to her, but this was not true. She played so loudly that the neighbors would complain. She played so hard that she would be covered with sweat. She never took a lesson, and she played horrendously. Yet, every single time she played, David would say how much better she was getting. He would never get angry or irritated with her. And that's what she was looking for. Any man that Valerie would consider marrying would have to be supportive of her and not get angry—no matter what. And she wasn't going to just believe them when they said they would support her no matter what. They had to prove it. That was the point.

Well, David passed the drum test, but Valerie had more up her sleeve. Next came the infamous chocolate chip test. Here's how it works: You get one bowl of chocolate chip ice cream with chocolate nuggets in it. You give it to him with a single spoon. Then you both sit down and watch TV. He, of course, will say, "Don't you want any?" You reply, "No, I'm not hungry." Then a few minutes later, point at the bowl and say, "Can I have that one chip, that big one?" Do this every few minutes. If he says, "Go get your own damn ice cream," he fails. But in David's case, he continued to give Valerie chip after chip after chip—as many as she wanted, all with a smile. Thus, he proved his generosity.

David didn't know he was being tested. Valerie told no one. In her heart, she didn't think he or anyone would pass even one of her tests, but she wasn't going to get married again and get hurt, and she was determined not to fall in love. She didn't trust love. Neither did David for that matter—they had both had bad first marriages. But this relationship was built on friendship, and neither of them liked being single either.

Next, Valerie went to a ceramic shop and bought a

huge ugly lion. It was meant to be carefully painted by hand. Valerie just poured an awful color of paint all over it. The clerks in the store thought Valerie was crazy to be making something so ugly. On the bottom, Valerie wrote "to David from Valerie." She left the monstrosity on his doorstep. She told him how hard she had worked on it. Despite his children's protests, David put it in his living room and said he loved it.

Whatever she did, David would support her. Valerie would cook a bad meal, and David would relish it. He passed all of the tests with flying colors. Four months after Valerie and David met, she knew she had better marry this man right away before somebody else figured out what a catch he was.

It was time for David to meet Valerie's parents and sister. Valerie and David drove four hours from California to Arizona in two separate cars with their children. Valerie's father was ultraconservative, and she couldn't risk having him think they were living together—even though they weren't.

They all met for a day picnic at the Colorado River, near where Valerie grew up. It was an exciting day. Valerie showed everyone how to water-ski. They boated and swam and rode motorcycles and ate ice cream. The only problem was Valerie's Dad, who kept snooping about and making it difficult for David and Valerie even to sneak a kiss.

That night, parked outside Valerie's family's house, David and Valerie were necking under the stars in David's truck. Her dad sneaked up behind them.

Before Valerie went inside, leaving David to sleep in the truck, she told him that he should marry her because she couldn't handle her father's shenanigans anymore and she couldn't handle dating either. He would have to either marry her or split up. Valerie calls this a "negative closing." It's a sales term. It means buy the product or lose it. She doesn't know what she would have done if he had said no, but he didn't. David's reaction was an immediate "OK." The next morning they announced their engagement.

It wasn't until a year after they were married that they actually spoke of love. And it was to be five years more before Valerie admitted she had tested David. She had to be sure the marriage was solid. He wasn't surprised, though, and he didn't mind. In fact he thinks it's kind of funny. And does he mind that she proposed? Not at all; it saved him the trouble, he says.